From Broken to Being

How Anyone Can Become the Highest Versions of Themselves Starting from Anywhere

Harry Jones III

Table of Contents

Developing emotional intelligence and self-awareness.

Mastering emotions and overcoming negative self-talk.

The role of visualization, affirmations, and attraction in shaping reality.

Reprogramming the subconscious mind for positive change.

Cultivating resilience and mental toughness.

The importance of seeking guidance and mentorship.

Chapter 3

Big Risk, Big Reward

The importance of taking calculated risks for growth.

Personal stories of taking big risks and the lessons learned.

Assessing risk and reward before making major decisions.

Overcoming fear and uncertainty associated with risk-taking.

The role of preparation and planning in mitigating risks.

Embracing failure as a learning opportunity.

Inspiring examples of individuals who achieved greatness through risk-taking.

The importance of having a support system and mentors.

Celebrating successes and learning from failures.

Chapter 4

Learning from Adversity

Reframing adversity as a catalyst for growth.

Personal reflections on overcoming challenges and setbacks.

Strategies for building resilience and strength through adversity.

The role of mindset and perspective in dealing with difficult situations.

Finding meaning and purpose in adversity.

The importance of self-compassion and forgiveness.

Turning pain into power and using experiences to help others.

Celebrating resilience and using adversity as a stepping stone to success.

Chapter 5
Finding True Purpose

The journey of self-discovery and finding one's true calling.

The importance of aligning passions and talents with purpose.

Overcoming societal expectations and pressures.

The role of intuition and inner guidance in discovering purpose.

Living a purpose-driven life and finding fulfillment.

The importance of continuous growth and evolution.

Chapter 6
Be Do Have

The Art of Being:

    The Biblical Principle of Be Do Have

    Creation and the First Commandment

    Becoming the Person Who Can Achieve Success

    High Frequency Chart

    Choosing Your Being

Doing the Work:

    The importance of consistent effort and dedication.

    Developing discipline and focus.

    Overcoming procrastination and self-doubt.

    The power of habits and routines in achieving goals.

    Extreme Dedication and Positive Daily Actions

    Challenging Negative Self-Talk and Delaying Gratification

The Haves and Have-Nots:

    Principles of Sowing and Reaping

    Developing an Abundance Mindset

    Overcoming scarcity mindset and limiting beliefs

    Building a legacy and leaving a positive impact

Summary
Acknowledgments

About The Harry Jones Group LLC,

Note to Readers

Hey there, fellow journeyers!

Ever felt like life's been throwing you curveballs since day one? Like you're constantly battling uphill, dodging obstacles, and questioning your purpose? Yeah, me too. My name is Harry, and this book isn't your typical self-help guide filled with fluffy promises and unrealistic expectations. It's a raw, unfiltered account of my journey – the messy, the painful, the exhilarating, and the downright transformative.

I won't sugarcoat it: life can be tough. I've faced financial struggles, racial prejudice, devastating losses, and even battled the demons of depression. But through it all, I've discovered a resilience within myself that I never knew

existed. I've learned that even in our darkest moments, we have the power to rise above, to heal, and to become the highest versions of ourselves.

This book is my personal journal, a collection of stories, lessons, and hard-won wisdom that I'm sharing with you. It's not about preaching from a pedestal; it's about having a real conversation, a heart-to-heart, about the challenges we face and the incredible potential we hold within.

So, what can you expect from these pages?

1. **Real Talk:** I'm not holding back. I'm sharing the nitty-gritty details of my life, the good, the bad, and the ugly. Why? Because I believe in the power of vulnerability and

authenticity. When we share our struggles, we connect with others on a deeper level and realize we're not alone.

2. **Practical Tools:** This isn't just a storybook. I'm giving you actionable strategies, tools, and techniques that I've used to overcome adversity, master my mind, and find my purpose. These are the same tools that have helped me transform my life, and I'm confident they can do the same for you.

3. **Spiritual Guidance:** My faith has been a guiding light throughout my journey. I'll be sharing the biblical principles and spiritual practices that have helped me find strength, hope, and direction. Whether you're a devout believer or simply curious about spirituality, I believe these principles can offer valuable insights for anyone seeking personal growth.

4. **A Dose of Inspiration:** Above all, I hope this book inspires you. I want you to see that no matter where you're starting from, no matter what you've been through, you have the power to create a life you love. You have the strength to overcome any obstacle, the resilience to bounce back from setbacks, and the potential to achieve your wildest dreams.

This book is for anyone who's ever felt broken, lost, or unsure of their path. It's for the dreamers, the doers, the seekers, and the survivors. It's for anyone who's ready to embark on a journey of self-discovery, healing, and transformation.

So, grab a cup of tea, get comfy, and let's dive in together. I'm excited to share my story with you, and I hope it sparks a fire within you to create your own extraordinary life.

Remember, it's never too late to start over, to reinvent yourself, to become the person you were always meant to be. This is your journey, and I'm honored to be a part of it.

Let's get started!

Your friend on this journey,

Harry Jones III

Introduction

In the tapestry of life, we are all artists, crafting our own unique masterpieces. Some strokes may be bold and vibrant, while others may be hesitant and muted. But every stroke, every color, every shade contributes to the intricate beauty of our individual stories.

This book is an invitation to embark on a journey of self-discovery, a quest to uncover the hidden depths of your being and unleash your full potential. It's a guide to navigating the twists and turns of life, to transforming challenges into opportunities, and to ultimately becoming the highest version of yourself.

My name is Harry Jones III, and I'm not your typical self-help guru. I'm a 23-year-old entrepreneur, speaker, and artist who's experienced more ups and downs than a rollercoaster. I've faced financial struggles, racial prejudice,

devastating losses, and even battled the demons of depression. But through it all, I've discovered a resilience within myself that I never knew existed.

I've learned that our past doesn't define us. It's not the cards we're dealt, but how we play them that matters. It's about taking ownership of our lives, embracing our challenges, and using them as fuel for growth.

In this book, I'll share my personal journey with you – the raw, unfiltered truth of my experiences. I'll talk about the setbacks that knocked me down, the lessons that lifted me up, and the mindset shifts that transformed my life.

But this book isn't just about me. It's about you. It's about empowering you to take charge of your own life, to overcome your obstacles, and to create a future that fills you with joy and purpose.

We'll explore the power of mindset, the importance of self-mastery, and the transformative potential of risk-taking. We'll delve into the biblical principle of "Be, Do, Have" and discover how it can guide us towards success in all areas of life.

We'll learn how to turn adversity into advantage, how to find our true purpose, and how to live a life of authenticity and honor.

This book is a call to action, a challenge to step outside your comfort zone and embrace the unknown. It's a reminder that you are capable of achieving anything you set your mind to, that you are worthy of love and happiness, and that you have a unique contribution to make to the world.

So, if you're ready to embark on a journey of self-discovery, if you're ready to unleash your full potential, if you're ready to create a life that lights you up from the inside out, then this book is for you.

Let's dive in together and discover the incredible power that lies within you.

Your journey starts now.

Chapter 1

The Journey of Harry Jones III

Buckle up, folks, because this is where the real story begins. I'm not talking about a fairy tale with a perfect ending. This is a raw, unfiltered account of my journey – a journey filled with twists, turns, and a whole lot of unexpected detours. It's a story about overcoming adversity, embracing challenges, and ultimately discovering the power that lies within each and every one of us.

I wasn't born with a silver spoon in my mouth. Far from it. I grew up in a small town, raised in a household where money was tight and dreams often felt out of reach. But even as a young boy, I had a fire burning inside of me, a relentless determination to create a better life for myself and my family.

That fire was tested time and time again. I faced racial prejudice, financial struggles, and the devastating loss of loved ones. There were times when I felt like giving up, like the weight of the world was too heavy to bear. But deep down, I knew I had a purpose, a calling that was bigger than my circumstances.

In this chapter, I'll take you on a journey through my childhood, adolescence, and early adulthood. We'll explore the defining moments that shaped me, the challenges that tested my resilience, and the turning points that led me to where I am today.

We'll talk about the power of perseverance, the importance of self-belief, and the transformative potential of taking risks. We'll delve into the role of faith,

family, and mentors in shaping our lives. And we'll discover how even the darkest moments can become catalysts for growth and transformation.

So, get ready to laugh, to cry, and to be inspired. This is my story, but it's also your story. It's a reminder that no matter where you've been or what you've faced, you have the power to overcome any obstacle and create a life that is truly extraordinary.

Early childhood experiences and challenges

My earliest memories are a whirlwind of emotions—joy, fear, confusion, and an unshakeable sense of love. Growing up Black in Doylestown, Pennsylvania, a predominantly white town, was like living in two worlds. One was filled with the warmth and vibrancy of my family, their laughter echoing through our home, the aroma of food filling the air. The other was a world of stark contrast, where I often felt like an outsider, my skin color a glaring difference in a sea of white faces.

Our family wasn't just one of the few Black families in Doylestown; we were also one of the less fortunate ones. My dad, a hardworking man with dreams of climbing the corporate ladder, struggled to make ends meet. My mom, the anchor of our family, poured her heart and soul into raising me and my four sisters.

Money was always tight, and we faced the constant threat of eviction, repossession, and bankruptcy.

I remember the anxiety that would wash over my father every time a bill collector called, the shame I felt when we had to rely on left overs and hand-me-downs. But amidst the struggle, there was also an undeniable sense of love and resilience. My parents, despite their hardships, always made sure we felt cherished and supported.

We may not have had the fanciest clothes or the latest gadgets, but we had something far more valuable: each other. We'd have impromptu dance parties in our living room, build forts out of blankets and pillows, and spend countless hours playing outside in the park. Those moments of joy and connection were like bright sparks in the darkness, reminding us that even in the midst of adversity, there was always something to be grateful for.

As I grew older, the challenges I faced became more complex. I became acutely aware of the racial prejudice that existed in our town. I was often the target of microaggressions, subtle slights that chipped away at my self-esteem. I was followed in stores, questioned by police, and treated with suspicion simply because of the color of my skin.

These experiences left me feeling angry, frustrated, and confused. I didn't understand why I was being treated differently, why I was being judged before I even had a chance to prove myself. It was during these times that I turned to football, a sport that became my refuge, my escape, and my source of identity.

On the football field, I felt like I belonged. I was part of a team, a brotherhood, where my skin color didn't matter. All that mattered was my skill, my dedication, and my willingness to push myself to the limit. Football taught me the importance of discipline, teamwork, and perseverance. It gave me a sense of purpose and direction when everything else in my life felt uncertain.

But even football couldn't shield me from the harsh realities of life. During my junior year of high school, I suffered a devastating knee injury that sidelined me for the rest of the season. It was a major setback, not just for my athletic aspirations but also for my sense of self. Football had been my ticket to a better future, my way out of poverty. Without it, I felt lost and adrift.

The following year, just as I recovered from my knee injury, I broke and tore the ligaments in my thumb in the first game of my senior season. Playing the rest of the season with the injury, yet It was another crushing blow for recruitment, one that shifted my dreams of playing college football and potentially making it to the NFL.

These injuries were more than just physical setbacks; they were emotional and psychological blows that left me questioning my identity and my purpose. I felt like I had lost a part of myself, a part that I had worked so hard to cultivate.

But even in the face of adversity, I refused to give up. I knew that I had to find a new path, a new way to express myself and make my mark on the world. And that's when I discovered my passion for art and custom sneakers.

Growing up in a financially disadvantaged household

Our home in Doylestown wasn't just a place to live; it was a microcosm of our family's struggles and triumphs. With four kids and two hardworking parents, space was always at a premium. We shared rooms, clothes, and even dreams, our lives intertwined in a way that forged an unbreakable bond.

Money was a constant worry, a dark cloud that hung over our household. My dad, a man of unwavering determination, worked tirelessly to provide for us. He'd leave before the sun rose and return long after it had set, his shoulders heavy with the weight of responsibility. My mom, the heart and soul of our family, stretched every dollar as far as it could go, her resourcefulness and creativity a testament to her love for us.

Despite their best efforts, the financial strain was relentless. The arrival of the mail was a mixed bag, sometimes bringing a glimmer of hope in the form of a paycheck, other times a crushing blow in the form of an overdue notice.

We lived paycheck to paycheck, our lives a constant juggling act of priorities. There were times when the lights would flicker, threatening to plunge us into darkness.

The holidays were particularly challenging. While other families reveled in abundance, we often had to make do with what we had. Hand-me-down gifts, toy drives, handmade decorations, and homemade dinners became our traditions, a testament to our resilience and ability to find joy in the simplest of things.

But even in the midst of hardship, there was an undeniable sense of love and togetherness in our home. My parents, despite their worries, always made sure we felt cherished and supported. They taught us the value of hard work, perseverance, and the importance of family.

We may not have had much in terms of material possessions, but we had something far more valuable: each other. We'd gather around the table for family dinners, sharing stories and laughter, our voices a symphony of love and resilience. We'd play board games on the floor, our competitive spirits igniting a fire that warmed our hearts. We'd huddle together on the couch, watching movies and sharing snacks, our bodies intertwined in a comforting embrace.

Those moments of connection and joy were like beacons of light in the darkness, reminding us that we were not defined by our circumstances. We were a family, united by love, strengthened by adversity, and determined to create a better future for ourselves.

Growing up in a financially disadvantaged household was undoubtedly challenging. It taught me the harsh realities of life at a young age, exposing me to the anxieties and insecurities that come with poverty. But it also instilled

in me a deep appreciation for the simple things in life, the importance of family, and the unwavering belief that with hard work and determination, anything is possible.

These early experiences shaped me into the person I am today, a resilient, resourceful, and compassionate individual who is committed to making a positive impact on the world. They taught me that true wealth is not measured by material possessions, but by the richness of our relationships, the strength of our character, and the depth of our love for others.

Experiencing racial prejudice and discrimination

As I navigated the complexities of adolescence, the sting of racial prejudice became an unwelcome companion. It wasn't always overt or malicious, but it was ever-present, lurking beneath the surface of everyday interactions. Microaggressions, those subtle slights and insults, were a constant reminder that I was different, that I didn't quite belong.

I remember the time I was 8 years old and my next door neighbor whom we hung out with all the time, called the police on me accusing me of stealing money and jewelry from her home. Having the police make me wait at the police car as He searched around until it was found hidden in their younger daughter's room. I went home that night feeling terrified and confused. I am only a kid, I thought they liked me..

Another time, I was walking to work in my purple planet fitness uniform when a police car pulled up beside me. The officer, a young white man, rolled down his window and asked me where I was going. I told him I was heading to work pointing at planet fitness straight ahead, but he didn't seem satisfied with my answer. He asked me a series of questions, his eyes scanning me up and down, as if searching for something incriminating.

I felt a knot of fear tighten in my stomach. I knew I hadn't done anything wrong, but the officer's demeanor made me feel like a criminal. After what felt like an eternity, he said "oh wrong guy" finally let me go and drove off, but the encounter left me shaken and angry.

These were just a few of the countless things I experienced growing up. They were like tiny paper cuts, each one individually insignificant, but collectively leaving a deep wound. They chipped away at my self-esteem, making me question my worth and my place in the world.

The weight of these experiences was compounded by the lack of representation I saw in my community. There were few Black role models in Doylestown, few people who looked like me and had achieved success. This lack of representation made it difficult for me to envision a future for myself beyond the limited options I saw around me.

I felt like I was constantly being told, both explicitly and implicitly, that my dreams were too big, that my aspirations were unrealistic. I was being boxed in by societal expectations, my potential stifled by the weight of prejudice.

But even in the face of these challenges, a fire burned within me. A fire fueled by a deep-seated desire to prove the naysayers wrong, to break free from the limitations imposed upon me, and to create a life that was truly my own.

This fire would eventually lead me on a journey of self-discovery, a journey that would take me through the darkest valleys and up to the highest peaks. It would be a journey filled with pain, loss, and adversity, but also with resilience, growth, and ultimately, triumph.

The experiences I faced during my childhood were undoubtedly painful, but they also served as a catalyst for my personal growth. They ignited a fire

within me, a determination to rise above the limitations imposed upon me and to create a life that was truly my own.

As I reflect on these experiences, I realize that they were not just personal challenges, but also reflections of a larger societal issue. Racism is a systemic problem that has plagued our country for centuries, and its effects are far-reaching and devastating.

It's important to acknowledge the pain and trauma that racism inflicts on individuals and communities. It's important to have honest conversations about race and to work towards creating a more equitable and just society for all.

But it's also important to remember that we are not defined by the circumstances and discrimination we face. We have the power to rise above it, to use our experiences as fuel for growth, and to create a better future for ourselves and for generations to come.

The impact of family dynamics on personal development.

Family, the cornerstone of our lives, the first chapter in our personal narratives. It's where we learn our first lessons, form our earliest bonds, and develop the foundation upon which we build our lives. My family, a vibrant tapestry of personalities, experiences, and challenges, has been instrumental in shaping the person I am today.

Growing up, our household was a whirlwind of activity. With four sisters and two parents under one roof, there was never a dull moment. Laughter, arguments, shared meals, and impromptu dancing filled our days. We are a close-knit bunch, bound together by love, shared experiences, and the unspoken understanding that we were all in this together.

My father, a man of few words but unwavering work ethic, instilled in me the importance of perseverance and dedication. He wasn't always around due to his demanding job, but his presence was felt in the sacrifices he made to provide for our family. He taught me the value of hard work, the importance of setting goals, and the power of never giving up on your dreams.

My mother, the heart and soul of our family, was a constant source of love, support, and encouragement. She was the glue that held us together, the one who always knew how to make us laugh, even in the toughest of times. She taught me the importance of compassion, empathy, and kindness. She showed me the power of unconditional love and the importance of cherishing family bonds.

My sisters, each with their own unique personalities and quirks, were my first friends, my confidantes, and my partners in crime. We share secrets, dreams, and countless adventures. They taught me the importance of loyalty, compromise, and the power of sisterhood.

But family dynamics are complex, and ours was no exception. Financial struggles cast a long shadow over our household, creating an undercurrent of stress and anxiety amongst other things. The constant worry about making ends meet, the fear of eviction, and relying on assistance took a toll on our emotional well-being.

These challenges, however, also brought us closer together. We learned to rely on each other for support, to find strength in our unity, and to celebrate the small victories. We discovered that even in the midst of adversity, love and laughter could still bloom.

The impact of family dynamics on personal development is undeniable. Our families shape our beliefs, values, and behaviors. They provide us with a

sense of identity, belonging, and purpose. They teach us how to navigate relationships, how to cope with challenges, and how to find our place in the world.

In my case, my family's financial struggles instilled in me a deep-seated desire for financial security and independence. The racial prejudice I witnessed firsthand fueled my determination to break down barriers and create a more equitable society. And the love and support I received from my family gave me the strength and resilience to overcome adversity and pursue my dreams.

As I reflect on my childhood experiences, I realize that my family, with all its complexities and challenges, has been the single most influential factor in my personal development. It has shaped me into the person I am today, a person who is passionate about empowering others, who is committed to making a positive impact on the world, and who is grateful for the lessons learned along the way.

The family is a microcosm of society, a reflection of the larger world we live in. By understanding the dynamics within our own families, we can gain valuable insights into the forces that shape our lives and the world around us. We can learn to appreciate the diversity of human experience, to empathize with others, and to work towards creating a more inclusive and compassionate society.

Discovering a passion for football and its role in shaping identity.

In the midst of the chaos and confusion of my early childhood, football emerged as a beacon of hope, a sanctuary where I could escape the harsh realities of my life and discover a sense of belonging and purpose. It wasn't just a sport; it was a lifeline, a way to channel my energy, my frustrations, and my dreams.

From the moment I first stepped onto the gridiron, I was hooked. The thrill of the game, the camaraderie of the team, the physicality of the sport—it all resonated with me on a deep level. Football became more than just a hobby; it became an integral part of my identity.

I dedicated myself to the sport with unwavering passion. I spent countless hours practicing, studying game film, and honing my skills. I dreamed of playing college football, of earning a scholarship, of making it to the NFL. Football wasn't just a game; it was my ticket to a better future, a way to break the cycle of poverty and create a life of opportunity for myself and my family.

The gridiron became my proving ground, a place where I could showcase my talent, my determination, and my resilience. Every tackle, every catch, every touchdown was a testament to my hard work and dedication. It was a way to silence the doubts and naysayers, to prove that I was more than just a statistic, more than just a product of my environment.

Football also provided me with a sense of belonging that I often lacked in other areas of my life. On the field, I was part of a team, a brotherhood, where my skin color didn't matter. All that mattered was my ability to contribute, to support my teammates, and to strive for a common goal.

The camaraderie I experienced on the football field was unlike anything I had ever known. We were a band of brothers, united by our love for the game and our shared commitment to excellence. We celebrated our victories together, mourned our losses together, and pushed each other to be the best we could be.

Through football, I learned the importance of discipline, teamwork, and perseverance. I learned how to set goals, how to overcome obstacles, and how to push myself beyond my limits. I learned the value of hard work, the importance of dedication, and the power of never giving up on your dreams.

But perhaps most importantly, football taught me the importance of believing in myself. It showed me that I was capable of achieving great things, that I had the potential to make a difference in the world. It gave me the confidence to pursue my dreams, even when the odds were stacked against me.

The impact of football on my personal development was profound. It shaped my values, my beliefs, and my aspirations. It taught me the importance of hard work, dedication, and teamwork. It gave me a sense of identity, belonging, and purpose.

But football also taught me about the harsh realities of life. It taught me about the pain of injury, the disappointment of defeat, and the importance of resilience in the face of adversity. It taught me that even our most cherished dreams can be shattered in an instant, and that it's how we respond to those setbacks that truly defines us.

As I reflect on my journey with football, I realize that it was more than just a sport. It was a transformative experience that shaped me into the person I am today. It taught me valuable life lessons that I continue to carry with me, lessons about perseverance, resilience, and the importance of believing in yourself.

Football may not have been my ultimate destiny, but it played a crucial role in shaping my identity and preparing me for the challenges and opportunities that lay ahead. It taught me that even when life throws you a curveball, you have the power to pick yourself up, dust yourself off, and keep moving forward.

Setbacks and injuries in high school.

High school, a time of self-discovery, growth, and for many, the pursuit of dreams. For me, it was the football field that held the promise of a brighter future. The roar of the crowd, the thrill of the game, the camaraderie of my teammates—it was my haven, my escape, my path to a college scholarship and maybe, just maybe, a shot at the NFL.

But life, as it often does, had other plans.

Junior year, the season was in full swing. The energy was electric, the stakes were high. We were facing off against Penridge, a fierce rival, and the adrenaline was pumping through my veins. As a cornerback, my job was to shut down the opposing team's wide receiver, and I was determined to do just that.

But in a split second, everything changed. As I jammed him off the line and he fell on his back pulling me down, I felt a sickening pop in my knee, a sharp pain that shot up my leg. I tried to shake it off, to push through the pain, but my body had other ideas. My knee kept clicking, and I knew something was seriously wrong. Playing the rest of the second half determined, or maybe stubborn, hobbling my way through I finished out strong.

The diagnosis was a torn meniscus, requiring surgery and months of rehabilitation. My dreams of a breakout junior season, of showcasing my skills to college recruiters, were shattered. It was a devastating blow, one that left me feeling lost and uncertain about my future.

But I refused to let this setback define me. With the support of my family, friends, and coaches, I embarked on a long and arduous journey of recovery. I spent countless hours in physical therapy, pushing my body to its limits, determined to regain my strength and agility.

The road to recovery was long and arduous, filled with setbacks and frustrations. There were days when I wanted to give up, when the pain seemed unbearable, when the doubt crept in. But I held onto the hope that I would one day return to the field, stronger and more determined than ever.

And finally, after months of hard work and dedication, I was cleared to play again. The feeling of stepping back onto the field, of hearing the roar of the crowd, of feeling the adrenaline surge through my veins—it was indescribable. It was a moment of triumph, a testament to the power of perseverance and the human spirit.

But my return to the field as a 4 way starter was short-lived. In the first game of my senior season, I suffered another devastating injury, this time to my hand. The pain was excruciating, but I refused to let it stop me. I taped up my hand, gritted my teeth, and played through the pain, determined to make the most of my final season.

But the injury took its toll. I was limited in my ability to play both offense and defense, and my performance suffered. The scholarship offers that had once seemed within reach began to dwindle, and my dreams of playing college football seemed to slip further and further away.

The setbacks and injuries I experienced in high school were more than just physical challenges. They were tests of my character, my resilience, and my determination. They forced me to confront my fears, my doubts, and my limitations.

But they also taught me valuable lessons about perseverance, about the importance of never giving up on your dreams, and about the power of the human spirit to overcome adversity. They showed me that even in the face of setbacks, there is always hope, always a chance to rise above and achieve greatness.

The loss of loved ones and its emotional toll.

The relentless march of time brought with it not only personal triumphs on the football field but also the heart-wrenching sting of loss. The bonds I had forged with friends and family were tested as the grim specter of death cast its shadow over my world.

It was a regular day at school, actually a few days before my birthday when I got the call to the principal's office that would forever alter the course of my life. My cousin, Matthew, had overdosed on Fentanyl. The news hit me like a punch to the gut, leaving me breathless and numb. Matthew, a vibrant soul with an infectious laugh and a heart of gold, had succumbed to the demons that had haunted him for years.

The pain was unbearable. I couldn't comprehend how someone so full of life could be gone so soon. I felt a profound sense of loss, a gaping hole in my heart that refused to heal. The world seemed dimmer, the colors less vibrant, the joy drained from my life.

Matthew's death was a wake-up call, a stark reminder of the fragility of life and the devastating consequences of addiction. It was a loss that shook me to my core, forcing me to confront my own mortality and the fleeting nature of our time on this earth.

But Matthew's passing was not the only loss I would endure. Just a few months prior, my close friend was tragically murdered. The news sent shockwaves through our world, leaving us reeling in disbelief and grief.

I remember the day I heard about his death. I was on my way to school, my mind wandering, when my phone buzzed with a text message. It was a friend, sharing the devastating news. I felt a wave of nausea wash over me, my heart pounding in my chest. I couldn't breathe, couldn't think, couldn't process the information.

I left school early that day, my mind racing, my heart aching. I walked home in a daze, the world around me a blur. I couldn't escape the images of my friend, his infectious smile, his kind heart, his dreams for the future.

The loss of these two people in such a short span of time was almost too much to bear. It felt like the universe was conspiring against me, testing my strength and resilience in the most cruel way imaginable.

The emotional toll of these losses was immense. I struggled with depression, anxiety, and a deep sense of emptiness. I felt like I was drowning in a sea of grief, unable to find my way back to the surface.

I turned to unhealthy coping mechanisms, seeking solace in substances and distractions. I tried to numb the pain, to escape the reality of my loss, but it was a futile attempt. The pain was always there, lurking beneath the surface, waiting to resurface at the most unexpected moments.

The loss of loved ones is a universal experience, one that touches every human life. It's a pain that cuts deep, a wound that takes time to heal. But even in the darkest of times, there is hope. There is the possibility of finding meaning in loss, of using our pain to fuel our growth, and of honoring the memory of those we've lost by living a life that is full of purpose and meaning.

For me, the loss of my friends was a turning point. It forced me to confront my own mortality, to re-evaluate my priorities, and to seek a deeper meaning in life. It was a catalyst for change, a spark that ignited a fire within me to live a life that would make my friends proud.

I realized that I couldn't let their deaths be in vain. I had to honor their memory by living a life that was true to myself, a life that was filled with passion, purpose, and service to others.

The pain of loss never truly goes away, but it can be transformed. It can be channeled into something positive, something that honors the memory of those we've lost and inspires us to live a life that is worthy of their legacy.

Discovering a passion for art and custom sneakers.

As the dust settled on my shattered football dreams, a new passion began to stir within me. It was a passion that would not only fill the void left by my athletic aspirations but also ignite a creative spark that would change the trajectory of my life.

During my recovery from thumb surgery, I found myself spending more and more time with my older sister, a talented artist studying at the University of the Arts in Philadelphia. I was drawn to her world of colors, textures, and self-expression. I watched in awe as she transformed blank canvases into vibrant masterpieces, her creations filled with emotion and creativity.

Inspired by her passion, I began to experiment with art myself. I started with tshirts, painting denim jackets, then I found myself drawn to the world of custom sneakers, fascinated by the idea of transforming ordinary shoes into unique works of art.

I spent hours researching different techniques, experimenting with different materials, and honing my skills. I watched countless YouTube tutorials, read articles and blogs, and sought advice from other custom sneaker artists. I was like a sponge, soaking up knowledge and eager to apply it to my own creations.

My first attempts were weak and amateurish, but I was unstoppable. I knew that with practice and dedication, I could improve. I spent countless hours in my bedroom, hunched over my desk, meticulously painting and customizing sneakers. I experimented with different designs, colors, and patterns, pushing the boundaries of my creativity.

As my skills improved, so did my confidence. I started wearing my custom sneakers to school, and they quickly caught the attention of my classmates. People started asking me to customize their shoes, and before I knew it, I had a small but growing clientele.

I decided to take my passion to the next level and started an Instagram account to showcase my work. I posted photos of my custom sneakers, along with behind-the-scenes glimpses of my creative process. The response was overwhelming. People from all over the world started following my account, liking and commenting on my posts.

I began receiving orders from people I had never met, from all walks of life. I customized sneakers for athletes, musicians, entrepreneurs, and everyday people who simply wanted to express their individuality through their footwear.

My passion for custom sneakers quickly evolved into a full-fledged business. I started investing in better materials, expanding my product line, and developing my brand. I was no longer just a hobbyist; I was an entrepreneur, a creator, a visionary.

The success of my business was exhilarating. I was making money doing something I loved, something that allowed me to express my creativity and connect with people from all over the world. It was a dream come true, a testament to the power of passion and perseverance.

But my journey as a custom sneaker artist was more than just a business venture. It was a form of self-expression, a way to channel my emotions, my experiences, and my unique perspective into tangible works of art. Each pair of sneakers I customized was a reflection of my soul, a piece of me that I shared with the world.

Through my art, I found a way to connect with others on a deeper level. I was able to tell stories, to evoke emotions, and to inspire others to express their own creativity. My custom sneakers became more than just footwear; they became symbols of individuality, self-expression, and empowerment.

The discovery of my passion for art and custom sneakers was a turning point in my life. It filled the void left by my shattered football dreams and gave me a new sense of purpose and direction. It taught me the importance of following my heart, of pursuing my passions, and of using my creativity to make a positive impact on the world.

But most importantly, it taught me the power of self-belief. It showed me that I was capable of achieving great things, even when the odds were stacked against me. It gave me the confidence to pursue my dreams, to embrace my unique talents, and to create a life that was truly my own.

Early entrepreneurial ventures and lessons learned.

The end of my football dreams didn't signal the end of my ambition; it simply redirected it. The energy that once fueled my athletic pursuits now found a new outlet: entrepreneurship. The spark was ignited by my newfound passion for art and custom sneakers, a creative endeavor that quickly blossomed into a business venture.

Fueled by youthful enthusiasm and a burning desire to succeed, I dove headfirst into the world of entrepreneurship. I started small, customizing sneakers for friends and family, but my ambition quickly outgrew my humble beginnings. I saw the potential to turn my passion into a profitable business, a way to not only express my creativity but also to achieve financial independence.

With the help of social media, I began to market my custom sneakers to a wider audience. I created an Instagram account to showcase my work, posting photos of my latest creations and engaging with potential customers. The response was overwhelming. Orders started coming in from all over the country, and I found myself working day and night to keep up with the demand.

The thrill of turning my passion into a profitable venture was intoxicating. I was making money doing something I loved, something that allowed me to express my creativity and connect with people from all walks of life. It was a dream come true, a testament to the power of hard work, dedication, and a little bit of entrepreneurial spirit.

But the road to entrepreneurial success was not without its bumps and detours. I quickly learned that running a business was more than just creating a great product; it was about marketing, customer service, financial management, and a whole host of other skills that I had to learn on the fly.

I made mistakes, plenty of them. I underpriced my products, over promised on delivery times, and struggled to manage my finances. There were times when I felt overwhelmed, stressed, and ready to throw in the towel.

But I also learned valuable lessons from these early entrepreneurial ventures. I learned the importance of setting realistic goals, of managing expectations, and of always striving to improve my skills and knowledge. I learned the value of customer feedback, the importance of building relationships, and the power of perseverance in the face of adversity.

One of the most important lessons I learned was the importance of financial management. I quickly realized that making money was only half the battle; the other half was knowing how to manage it. I had to learn how to budget, how to track expenses, and how to invest my profits wisely.

I also learned the importance of building a strong support system. I was fortunate to have family and friends who believed in me and my vision. They offered me guidance, encouragement, and a shoulder to lean on when things got tough.

My early entrepreneurial ventures were a rollercoaster ride of highs and lows, of triumphs and setbacks. But through it all, I learned valuable lessons that would serve me well in the years to come. I discovered the importance of passion, perseverance, and the willingness to learn from my mistakes.

These early experiences laid the foundation for my future entrepreneurial endeavors. They taught me the importance of having a clear vision, a solid plan, and the resilience to overcome challenges. They showed me that success is not a destination, but a journey, one that requires constant learning, adaptation, and growth.

Moving to Charlotte, North Carolina, and facing new challenges.

With a heart full of hope and a head full of dreams, I embarked on a new chapter in my life: a move to Charlotte, North Carolina. The decision was fueled by a mix of ambition, love, and the desire for a fresh start. My custom sneaker business was gaining traction, and I had fallen head over heels for a lady who had captured my heart. The prospect of building a life together in a new city, away from the familiar struggles of our past, was both exhilarating and terrifying.

Charlotte, with its vibrant energy and burgeoning art scene, seemed like the perfect place to nurture my entrepreneurial spirit and artistic aspirations. I envisioned myself creating a thriving business, connecting with a diverse community of artists and creatives, and building a life filled with love, laughter, and abundance.

The move itself was a whirlwind of packing, saying goodbyes, and embarking on a cross-country road trip with my girlfriend. As we drove south, I couldn't help but feel a mix of excitement and trepidation. I was leaving behind the familiar comforts of home, the support system of my family and friends, and the only life I had ever known.

But I was also filled with a sense of adventure, a yearning for new experiences and challenges. I was ready to embrace the unknown, to test my limits, and to see what this new chapter had in store for me.

The initial months in Charlotte were a blur of activity. I was working tirelessly to establish my business, networking with potential clients, and exploring the city's vibrant art scene. I was also adjusting to life as a partner and a bonus father figure to my girlfriend's daughter. It was a lot to handle, but I was determined to make it work.

However, the challenges of starting a new life in a new city quickly became apparent. The cost of living was higher than I had anticipated, and my income from the sneaker business was sporadic at best. I found myself struggling to make ends meet, juggling bills, and constantly worrying about money.

The pressure to succeed weighed heavily on my shoulders. I felt like I had to prove myself, not just to my girlfriend and her daughter, but also to myself and the world. I had left everything behind to pursue my dreams, and I couldn't bear the thought of failing.

The stress of financial instability began to take a toll on my mental health. I found myself withdrawing from my loved ones, spending hours alone in my studio, consumed by self-doubt and anxiety. The vibrant energy of Charlotte that had initially attracted me now felt overwhelming and suffocating.

To make matters worse, a fire broke out in our apartment complex, forcing us to evacuate and leaving our belongings damaged and destroyed. It was a devastating blow, one that added to the mounting pile of challenges I was already facing.

We were forced to move in with my sister, a cramped and uncomfortable situation that further strained our relationship. The dream of building a life together in Charlotte was quickly unraveling, replaced by a harsh reality of financial hardship and emotional turmoil.

The setbacks and challenges I faced in Charlotte were a far cry from the idyllic life I had envisioned. The dream of a thriving business, a loving family, and a vibrant social life seemed like a distant memory. I felt like I was drowning in a sea of adversity, struggling to keep my head above water.

But even in the midst of this storm, a flicker of hope remained. I knew that I couldn't give up, that I had to find a way to overcome these challenges and create a better future for myself and my loved ones. I had to dig deep, tap into my resilience, and find the strength to keep moving forward.

The fire in the apartment complex and its consequences.

Life in Charlotte had been a whirlwind of emotions, a constant juggling act between the highs of newfound love and the lows of financial strain. Just when I thought we had finally found our footing, fate dealt us another blow – a literal one.

It was a seemingly ordinary evening. We had all just fallen asleep in bed watching a movie, when we heard a commotion outside.

At first, we dismissed it as nothing out of the ordinary. But as the noise grew louder, we decided to investigate. We opened our front door to a scene of chaos. Smoke billowed from the apartment next door, and panicked residents were rushing out of the building.

The acrid smell of smoke filled the air, water pouring in the ceiling and a sense of dread washed over us. We grabbed our phones and a few essential belongings, grabbed my bonus daughter and rushed out of the apartment, running down the stairs passing the firefighters going up.

As we stood on the sidewalk, watching them destroy our home, a wave of despair washed over me. Everything we owned, everything we had worked so hard for, was going up in smoke. The dream of building a life together in Charlotte seemed to be crumbling before our eyes.

The fire department arrived quickly, but the damage was already done. Our apartment, along with several others, was completely destroyed. We were left with nothing but the clothes on our backs and the few belongings we had managed to grab in our haste.

The aftermath of the fire was a blur of phone calls, insurance claims, and frantic searches for temporary housing. We were forced to rely on the kindness of family and friends, bouncing from one couch to another, our belongings scattered in storage units and our suitcases.

The loss of our home was more than just a material setback; it was a devastating emotional blow. Our apartment had been our sanctuary, our safe haven, the place where we had hoped to build a future together. Now, it was nothing but memories.

The dream of building a life together in Charlotte was quickly unraveling, replaced by a harsh reality of loss, displacement, and emotional turmoil. The fire had not only destroyed our home; it had also shattered our illusions of stability and security.

In the aftermath of the fire, I found myself questioning everything. I questioned my decision to move to Charlotte, my ability to provide for my family, and my worth as a partner and a father figure. I felt like a failure, a burden, a disappointment.

The emotional toll of the fire was immense. I struggled with depression, anxiety, and a deep sense of hopelessness. I felt like I was trapped in a dark tunnel, with no light at the end.

But even in the midst of this darkness, a flicker of resilience remained. I knew that I couldn't let this setback define me. I had to find a way to rise from the ashes, to rebuild my life, and to create a better future for myself and my loved ones.

The fire in the apartment complex was a turning point in my life. It was a devastating loss, one that tested my strength and resilience to the limit. But it also taught me valuable lessons about the impermanence of material possessions, the importance of cherishing relationships, and the power of the human spirit to overcome adversity.

Financial struggles and the impact on mental health.

The initial excitement of our new life in Charlotte began to wane as the harsh realities of financial instability set in. The cost of living was higher than we had anticipated, and my income from the custom sneaker business was far from consistent. Some months were good, with a flurry of orders and a decent profit, but others were lean, leaving us scrambling to cover our basic expenses.

The weight of financial responsibility pressed down on me like a heavy boulder. I felt like I was constantly running on a treadmill, working tirelessly just to stay afloat. The dream of financial freedom, of building a comfortable life for my girlfriend and her daughter, seemed to slip further and further away.

The stress of our financial situation began to seep into every aspect of our lives. It manifested in sleepless nights, tense conversations, and a growing sense of despair. The joy and excitement that had once filled our days were replaced by worry, anxiety, and a fear of the future.

I found myself withdrawing from my loved ones, seeking solace in my work, but even that provided little relief. The pressure to succeed, to provide, to be

the man I had promised to be, was suffocating. I felt like I was failing, not just as an entrepreneur, but as a partner and a father figure.

The constant worry about money took a toll on my mental health. I started experiencing symptoms of depression – a persistent sadness, a loss of interest in activities I once enjoyed, and a feeling of hopelessness that seemed to permeate every aspect of my life.

I tried to hide my struggles from my girlfriend, not wanting to burden her with my worries. But the strain was evident in my demeanor, my actions, and in the way I withdrew into myself.

The financial struggles we faced were not just a practical problem; they were an emotional and psychological burden that threatened to tear us apart. The dream of building a life together was becoming a nightmare, a constant battle against the rising tide of debt and despair.

The impact of financial stress on mental health is well-documented. Studies have shown that financial worries can lead to a range of mental health problems, including depression, anxiety, and even suicidal ideation. The constant pressure to make ends meet, the fear of losing one's home or job, and the shame of not being able to provide for one's family can take a devastating toll on one's emotional well-being.

In my case, the financial struggles I faced exacerbated my existing vulnerabilities and triggered a downward spiral into depression. I felt trapped, helpless, and alone. I began to question my self-worth, my abilities, and my purpose in life.

The financial struggles I faced in Charlotte were a turning point in my life. They pushed me to the brink of despair, forcing me to confront my deepest fears and insecurities. But they also served as a catalyst for change, a wake-up call that led me to seek help and to embark on a journey of healing and self-discovery.

The descent into depression and thoughts of suicide.

The vibrant tapestry of my life, woven with threads of ambition, love, and creativity, began to unravel as the weight of accumulated setbacks and disappointments bore down on me. The fire in our apartment complex had been a devastating blow, leaving us homeless and financially strained. The dream of a thriving business and a happy family life in Charlotte seemed to slip further and further away.

The stress and uncertainty of our situation took a toll on my mental health. My physical health and relationships. The once vibrant colors of my life seemed to fade into a dull gray, and a heavy blanket of despair settled over me.

I turned to unhealthy coping mechanisms, seeking temporary relief in substances and distractions. I smoked weed excessively, hoping to numb the pain and escape the harsh realities of my life. But the relief was fleeting, and the guilt and shame that followed only deepened my despair.

My sleep patterns became erratic. I would stay up all night, consumed by negative thoughts and self-doubt, only to crash into a restless sleep filled with nightmares and anxieties. I neglected my physical health, eating poorly and neglecting exercise. My once vibrant energy dwindled, replaced by lethargy and apathy.

My relationship with my girlfriend suffered as well. The stress and strain of our situation created a rift between us. We argued more frequently, our communication broke down, the light in her eyes for me dimmed and the love that had once been our anchor seemed to drift further and further away.

I felt like a failure, a burden to my loved ones, a disappointment to myself. The dreams I had once held so dear seemed like distant memories, replaced by a bleak and hopeless future.

The descent into depression was gradual, insidious, like a slow-moving fog that gradually obscured my vision and clouded my judgment. I lost interest in everything.

The world around me seemed to lose its color, its vibrancy, its meaning. I felt like I was trapped in a dark tunnel, with no light at the end. The pain was relentless, suffocating, and I couldn't see a way out.

In the depths of my despair, the unthinkable becomes thinkable. The idea of ending my life, once a distant and abhorrent thought, now seemed like a viable escape from the torment I was enduring.

I remember the day I decided to end it all. I had just dropped my girlfriend off at work, and as I drove home, a wave of hopelessness washed over me. I couldn't bear the thought of facing another day of pain, of disappointment, of feeling like a failure.

Once I got home , my hands trembling, my heart pounding in my chest. I reached for my notepad and started writing goodbye letters to my loved ones. I apologized for my shortcomings, not being enough, for the pain I had caused, for the burden I had been.

As I wrote, tears streamed down my face, blurring the words on the paper. I felt a profound sense of emptiness, a void that couldn't be filled. I was ready to give up, to surrender to the darkness that had consumed me.

But as I drove to where I planned on taking my life, on the precipice of despair, I saw a few signs then something shifted within me. A small voice, barely a whisper, spoke to me. It reminded me of my strength, my resilience, my purpose. It told me that I was loved, that I was needed, that I had so much more to give to the world.

In that moment, I made a choice. I chose to fight. I chose to live. I chose to believe that there was still hope, that I could overcome this darkness and find my way back to the light.

The turning point: realizing the need for change and taking control of life.

The darkness had become all-consuming. It was a suffocating weight that pressed down on me, stealing my breath, my joy, my very will to live. The world had lost its color, its vibrancy, its meaning. I was a ghost of my former self, a hollow shell drifting through life without purpose or direction.

The pain was relentless, a gnawing ache that permeated every fiber of my being. It was a physical manifestation of the emotional turmoil that raged within me. I couldn't eat, I couldn't sleep, I couldn't find solace in anything.

The thought of suicide, once a distant whisper, now roared in my ears, a siren song promising an end to the suffering. I had written my goodbye letters, my final words to the people I loved. I had planned my exit, my escape from the unbearable weight of existence.

But as I sat on the edge of my bed, staring into the abyss, a flicker of something stirred within me. It was a faint glimmer of hope, a tiny spark of defiance against the darkness that threatened to consume me.

In that moment, I realized that I had a choice. I could succumb to despair, surrender to the darkness, and end my life. Or I could fight back, claw my way out of the abyss, and reclaim my life.

The choice was clear, but the path was not. I knew that I couldn't continue down the same destructive path. I had to make a change, a radical shift in my mindset and my actions.

I started by seeking help. I studied mentors, talked with trusted friends, and most importantly The Most High God. I opened up about my struggles, my pain, my fears. It was a vulnerable and humbling experience, but it was also incredibly liberating.

Through self work, I began to understand the root of my depression, the underlying traumas and unresolved issues that had been festering beneath the surface. I learned tools to manage my anxiety and negative thoughts.

They offered a listening ear, a shoulder to cry on, and unwavering support. Reminding me of my strengths, my resilience, and my potential. Helping me to see that I was not alone, that there were people who need me and wanted to see me succeed.

I've been guided back to my faith, reminding me of the power of prayer, wisdom, and connection to The Most High God. This helped me to find meaning in my suffering, to see it as an opportunity for growth and transformation.

With this support, I began to make small but significant changes in my life. I started working out regularly, eating healthier, and learning more skills. I reconnected with my passions, in building business and inspiring others.

I also started practicing gratitude, focusing on the blessings in my life rather than the challenges. I made a conscious effort to surround myself with positive people and to engage in activities that challenge me or bring me joy.

The road to recovery was not easy. There were setbacks, moments of doubt, and days when the darkness seemed to creep back in. But I persevered, drawing strength from my support system, my faith, and my newfound commitment to self-mastery.

As I slowly emerged from the depths of depression, I realized that I had been given a second chance at life. I had been through the fire and come out on the other side, stronger and more resilient than ever before.

I knew that I had a purpose, a reason for being here. I had a story to share, a message of hope and resilience to offer to others who were struggling.

And so, I made a decision. I decided to dedicate my life to helping others overcome adversity and achieve their full potential. I founded the Harry Jones Group, LLC. an education company focused on strategic education and emotional wellness.

Through speaking engagements, workshops, and online resources, I share my story and the lessons I've learned along the way. I teach others the tools and techniques that helped me overcome depression, anxiety, and addiction. I empower them to take control of their lives, to embrace their challenges, and to create a future that is filled with joy, purpose, and meaning.

The turning point in my life was not a single event, but a series of choices and actions that led me out of the darkness and into the light. It is a journey of self-discovery, healing, and transformation.

It is a journey that taught me the importance of seeking help, of building a strong support system, and of taking responsibility for my own life. It was a journey that showed me the power of the human spirit to overcome adversity and to create a life of purpose and meaning.

Rediscovering personal development, faith, and the importance of a positive mindset.

The moment I chose life over death was a turning point, a pivotal moment that marked the beginning of my journey back from the abyss. It was a decision born out of desperation, a flicker of hope amidst the darkness that had consumed me. But it was also a decision that would change the trajectory of my life.

In the aftermath of my suicide thoughts, I realized that I couldn't continue down the same destructive path. I had to make a change, a radical shift in my mindset and my actions. I knew that I needed to find a way to heal, to rebuild my life, and to rediscover my purpose.

My journey of rediscovery began with a renewed focus on personal development. I started reading the bible in depth, other books, listening to podcasts, and attending seminars on topics like self-improvement, mindset, and spirituality. I was hungry for knowledge, eager to learn anything that could help me understand myself and my place on this earth.

One of the first books I read was "Think and Grow Rich" by Napoleon Hill. The book's message of self-belief, positive thinking, and the power of the subconscious mind resonated with me deeply. It was as if Hill was speaking directly to me, offering a roadmap out of the darkness and into the light.

I also delved into the works of others like John C Maxwell, and Steve Siebold. Their teachings helped me to understand the power of my thoughts and beliefs, the importance of taking responsibility for my life, and the transformative potential of living in the present moment.

As I immersed myself in the world of personal development, I began to see my life through a new lens. I realized that I had been the architect of my own suffering, that my negative thoughts and beliefs had created a self-fulfilling prophecy of despair.

I learned that I had the power to change my thoughts, to reframe my experiences, and to create a new reality for myself. I discovered that I was not a victim of my circumstances, but a co-creator of my life.

Along with my newfound passion for personal development, I also reconnected with my faith. I had grown up with a zeal for God, but my faith had taken a backseat during my struggles with depression and addiction not following the ways and principles of God.

Now, I turned to the Bible for guidance and solace. I read the scriptures, prayed, and sought the counsel of my spiritual mentors. I found comfort in the words of God, who taught about strength, personal excellence, and the importance of living a life of purpose.

My faith gave me a sense of hope and meaning that I had been lacking. It reminded me that I was not alone, that I was fearfully and wonderfully made, and that I had a purpose to fulfill in this world.

As I continued on my journey of personal development and spiritual growth, I began to cultivate a more positive mindset. I learned to challenge my negative thoughts, to focus on growth, and to see the good in every situation.

I started practicing affirmations, repeating positive statements about myself and my life. I visualized myself achieving my goals, feeling the joy and fulfillment that would come with success. I surrounded myself with positive people who taught, uplifted and inspired me.

The shift in my mindset was gradual, but it was undeniable. I started to feel lighter, happier, and more optimistic about the future. The darkness that had once consumed me began to lift, replaced by a newfound sense of hope and possibility.

Rediscovering personal development, faith, and the importance of a positive mindset and actions was a turning point in my life. It was a journey of self-discovery, healing, and transformation. It was a journey that taught me the power of my thoughts, the importance of taking responsibility for my life, and the transformative potential of faith and spirituality.

This journey is ongoing, and I continue to learn and grow every day. But the lessons I've learned have empowered me to overcome adversity, to find my purpose, and to create a life that is filled with joy, meaning, and fulfillment.

The creation of the Harry Jones Group and its mission to empower youth.

Emerging from the depths of despair, I found myself standing on the precipice of a new beginning. The trials and tribulations I had endured had forged me into a stronger, more resilient individual. The pain, the loss, the struggles—they had all served a purpose, shaping me into the person I was meant to be.

I realized that my experiences, as painful as they were, had given me a unique perspective, a deep understanding of the human condition. I had walked through the fire and emerged on the other side, scarred but not broken. I had a story to tell, a message of hope and resilience to share with the world.

And so, The Harry Jones Group was born. It isn't just a business venture; it is a calling, a mission to empower people who are facing similar challenges to the ones I had overcome. I wanted to create a space where they could find support, guidance, and inspiration to navigate the complexities of life strategically.

The Harry Jones Group is more than just an education company; it's a movement, a community of individuals committed to personal growth, emotional resilience, and positive change. Our mission is to equip young people with the tools and resources they need to thrive in today's world.

We offer a variety of programs and services, including workshops, seminars, online courses, and one-on-one coaching. Our curriculum covers a wide range of topics, from self-awareness and character building to goal setting and leadership development.

But at the heart of The Harry Jones Group is a simple message: You are not alone. You are capable of achieving great things. You have the power to overcome any obstacle and create a life you love.

We believe that every person deserves the opportunity to reach their full potential. We believe that by providing them with the right tools and support, we can empower them to overcome adversity, achieve their dreams, and make a positive impact on the world.

The creation of The Harry Jones Group was a deeply personal endeavor. It is a way for me to give back, to use my experiences to help others. It is a way to honor the memory of my friends who had lost their lives to addiction and violence.

I'm pouring my heart and soul into the company, working tirelessly to develop myself, programs and resources that would make a real difference in the lives of the people. I speak at schools, community centers, and youth organizations, sharing my story and inspiring others to believe in themselves.

The response was overwhelming. Young people from all walks of life resonated with my message of hope and resilience. They saw themselves in my story, and they were inspired to take action and create positive change in their own lives.

The Harry Jones Group has been growing since its inception. We have reached people across the country, empowering them to overcome challenges, discover their passions, and create a brighter future for themselves.

But our work is far from over. We are constantly striving to expand our reach, to develop new programs and resources, and to create a more inclusive and supportive community for all.

The Harry Jones Group is more than just a company; it's a family, a movement, a beacon of hope for young people who are struggling to find their way. We are committed to empowering the next generation of leaders, innovators, and changemakers.

We believe that by investing in our youth, we are investing in the future of our communities and our world. We believe that by empowering young people to believe in themselves, we can create a brighter, more equitable, and more compassionate world for all.

CHAPTER 2

MASTERING YOUR MIND

Have you ever felt like your mind is completely against you, going off in a million different directions at once? Thoughts racing, worries swirling, doubts creeping in? If so, you're not alone. Our minds are incredibly powerful tools, capable of both incredible creativity and debilitating anxiety. But here's the secret: you are not your thoughts. You are the master of your mind, the captain of your ship, the architect of your reality.

In this chapter, we're diving deep into the fascinating world of the mind, exploring its intricate workings, its hidden powers, and the practical strategies you can use to harness its full potential. We'll uncover the secrets of abundance vs. scarcity mindset, the importance of controlling the controllables, and the transformative power of emotional intelligence.

This isn't just about positive thinking or wishful dreaming. It's about rewiring your brain for success, building mental resilience, and mastering your emotions so you can navigate life's challenges with grace and confidence.

We'll draw wisdom from biblical stories and spiritual principles, tapping into the ancient wisdom that has guided humanity for centuries. We'll also explore cutting-edge techniques like visualization, affirmations, and subconscious reprogramming, giving you a toolkit of practical strategies to upgrade your mental software.

Whether you're struggling with negative self-talk, battling limiting beliefs, or simply seeking to enhance your mental performance, this chapter is your guide to mastering your mind and unlocking your full potential.

Get ready to embark on a journey of self-discovery, to break free from the chains of fear and doubt, and to step into your power as the master of your own mind. This is where the real transformation begins.

Understanding the power of thoughts and beliefs.

Our minds are extraordinary tools, capable of both incredible creation and devastating destruction. They shape our perceptions, influence our emotions, and ultimately determine the course of our lives. Yet, for many of us, our minds remain an enigma, a vast and unexplored territory filled with untapped potential.

In the realm of personal development, understanding the power of thoughts and beliefs is paramount. Our thoughts are not mere fleeting notions; they are the seeds from which our reality grows. They shape our perceptions, influence our emotions, and ultimately determine the course of our lives.

Consider this: every action, every decision, every achievement, and every failure begins with a thought. Our thoughts are the architects of our reality, the blueprints upon which we build our lives.

If we believe we are capable, we are more likely to take risks and pursue our dreams. If we believe we are worthy, we are more likely to attract love and abundance into our lives. And if we believe we are destined for greatness, we are more likely to achieve it.

But the opposite is also true. If we harbor negative thoughts and limiting beliefs, we create self-fulfilling prophecies of failure and disappointment. We sabotage our own success, hold ourselves back from reaching our full potential, and create a reality that is far from what we truly desire.

The good news is that we have the power to change our thoughts and beliefs. We are not victims of our minds; we are their masters. By becoming aware of our thought patterns, challenging our limiting beliefs, and cultivating a positive mindset, we can transform our lives from the inside out.

One of the most powerful tools for mastering our minds is the practice of mindfulness. Mindfulness is the practice of paying attention to the present

moment without judgment. It involves observing our thoughts and feelings without getting caught up in them, allowing us to gain a deeper understanding of our inner world.

Through mindfulness, we can become aware of the negative thought patterns that hold us back. We can learn to challenge these thoughts, to question their validity, and to replace them with more positive and empowering beliefs.

Another powerful tool for transforming our thoughts and beliefs is the practice of affirmations. Affirmations are positive statements that we repeat to ourselves, either silently or aloud. By repeating affirmations regularly, we can reprogram our subconscious mind and create new neural pathways that support our desired outcomes.

For example, if you struggle with self-doubt, you might repeat affirmations like "I am worthy," "I am capable," or "I am enough." By consistently affirming these positive beliefs, you can gradually shift your mindset and create a more positive self-image.

The power of thoughts and beliefs extends beyond our individual lives. Our collective thoughts and beliefs shape our families, communities, societies, and our world. When we choose to focus on honor, love, compassion, and unity, we create a ripple effect that can transform the world around us.

But when we allow fear, hatred, and division to dominate our thoughts, we create a reality that is filled with conflict, suffering, and despair.

The choice is ours. We can choose to be victims of our minds, or we can choose to be their masters. We can choose to let our thoughts and beliefs control us, or we can choose to control them.

By understanding the power of our thoughts and beliefs, we can unlock our full potential and create a life that is truly extraordinary. We can overcome our challenges, achieve our dreams, and make a positive impact on the world.

The journey of mastering our minds is not always easy, but it is one of the most rewarding journeys we can embark on. It is a journey that leads to greater self-awareness, inner peace, and ultimately, a life of purpose and fulfillment.

The abundance vs. scarcity mindset and its impact on success.

Our minds are powerful tools, capable of shaping our reality and influencing our outcomes. The way we perceive the world, the beliefs we hold, and the thoughts we entertain can either propel us towards success or hold us back in a cycle of lack and limitation. One of the most critical distinctions in this mental landscape is the contrast between an abundance mindset and a scarcity mindset.

Understanding the Abundance Mindset

An abundance mindset is a belief in the limitless possibilities that life has to offer. It's a deep-seated conviction that there is enough for everyone, that opportunities are abundant, and that success is not a zero-sum game. People with an abundance mindset see challenges as opportunities for growth, setbacks as temporary detours, and failures as valuable learning experiences.

This mindset is characterized by generosity, gratitude, and a willingness to share knowledge and resources. It's about focusing on what you have, rather than what you lack, and believing that you are capable of achieving your goals and dreams.

The Scarcity Mindset: A Self-Fulfilling Prophecy

In contrast, a scarcity mindset is rooted in fear and lack. It's a belief that resources are limited, that opportunities are scarce, and that success comes at the expense of others or something. People with a scarcity mindset tend to be competitive, insecure, fleeting, and focused on protecting what they have.

This mindset can become a self-sabotaging prophecy. When you believe that there isn't enough to go around, you're more likely to hoard resources, miss out on opportunities, and sabotage your own success. You may also find yourself constantly comparing yourself to others, feeling envious of their achievements, and doubting your own abilities.

The Impact on Success

The abundance vs. scarcity mindset can have a profound impact on our personal and professional lives. People with an abundance mindset are more likely to take risks, pursue their passions, and build strong relationships. They are also more resilient in the face of adversity, seeing setbacks as temporary obstacles rather than insurmountable barriers.

On the other hand, a scarcity mindset can lead to a fear of failure, a reluctance to take risks, and a tendency to settle for less than we deserve. It can also create a toxic environment of competition and comparison, where we constantly feel like we're not good enough.

Shifting Your Mindset

The good news is that our mindsets are not fixed. We can choose to cultivate an abundance mindset, even if we've been conditioned to think in terms of scarcity. It starts with awareness – recognizing the negative thought patterns and limiting beliefs that are holding us back.

Once we become aware of our scarcity mindset, we can start to challenge and reframe those beliefs. We can practice gratitude, focusing on the abundance that already exists in our lives. We can celebrate the successes of others, rather than feeling threatened by them. We can embrace collaboration and cooperation, recognizing that we can achieve more together than we can alone.

My Journey from Scarcity to Abundance

Growing up in a financially disadvantaged household, I was conditioned to think in terms of scarcity. I believed that money was hard to come by, that opportunities were limited, and that success was reserved for the privileged few.

This scarcity mindset held me back for years. I was afraid to take risks, I doubted my abilities, and I settled for less than I deserved. It wasn't until I hit rock bottom, facing financial ruin and was exposed to what could be, that's when I realized the need for a change.

Through personal development, spiritual guidance, and hardwork, I began to shift my mindset from scarcity to abundance. I started to believe in my own potential, to see opportunities where I had once seen limitations, and to embrace a spirit of generosity and gratitude.

This shift in mindset had a profound impact on my life. I started taking calculated risks, pursuing my passions, and building meaningful relationships. I also became more resilient in the face of adversity, seeing setbacks as opportunities for growth rather than reasons to give up.

The abundance mindset has been instrumental in my entrepreneurial journey. It has allowed me to attract opportunities, build a growing business, and begin to create a life of abundance and fulfillment.

The Power of Choice

The choice between an abundance mindset and a scarcity mindset is yours to make. You can choose to live in fear and lack, or you can choose to embrace the limitless possibilities that life has to offer.

Remember, your mindset is not fixed. You have the power to change it, to rewire your brain for abundance, and to create a life that is truly extraordinary.

The importance of controlling the controllables.

In the grand scheme of life, there's a whole lot we can't control. The weather, the economy, other people's opinions—these are all things that are largely outside of our influence. It's easy to get caught up in the chaos and uncertainty of the world, to feel overwhelmed and powerless in the face of forces beyond our control.

But here's the thing: there's also a whole lot we can control. Our thoughts, our actions, our reactions, our choices—these are all within our sphere of influence. And it's in focusing on these controllables that we find our power, our dominion, and our ability to create the life we desire.

During my darkest moments, when depression had its grip on me and the weight of the world felt unbearable, I realized that I had been focusing on all the wrong things. I had been obsessing over the things I couldn't control, the setbacks, the losses, the unfairness of it all.

But in that moment of despair, a glimmer of clarity emerged. I realized that I had been giving away my power, my dominion, by focusing on the uncontrollable. I had been letting external circumstances dictate my internal state, allowing the chaos of the world to consume me.

I knew that I had to shift my focus, to reclaim my power by concentrating on the things I could control. I started with my thoughts. I became aware of the negative self-talk that had become my constant companion, the voice that told me I was a failure, a burden, a disappointment.

I challenged those thoughts, replacing them with positive affirmations and empowering beliefs. I reminded myself of my strengths, my resilience, and my potential. I focused on gratitude, appreciating the blessings in my life, no matter how small.

As I shifted my thoughts, my feelings began to shift as well. The heavy blanket of despair that had been suffocating me started to lift. I felt a renewed sense of hope, a glimmer of optimism that had been absent for so long.

With a more positive mindset, I began to take control of my actions. I started working out regularly, eating healthier, and growing my capacity through education. I reconnected with my passions, creating, building business, and inspiring others.

I also started setting goals, small achievable steps that would move me closer to my dreams. I focused on the things I could do, the actions I could take, to create a better future for myself.

As I took control of my thoughts and actions, I began to see a change in my circumstances. The world didn't magically transform overnight, but my perspective did. I was no longer a victim of my circumstances; I was an active participant in my life, shaping my reality through my choices and actions.

The importance of controlling the controllables cannot be overstated. It's a fundamental principle of personal development, a key to unlocking our full potential and creating a life of meaning and fulfillment.

When we focus on the things we can control, we empower ourselves. We take ownership of our lives, our choices, and our destinies. We become the masters of our fate, rather than the victims of our circumstances.

Controlling the controllables is not about denying the existence of challenges or pretending that everything is always perfect. It's about recognizing that we have a choice in how we respond to those challenges. We can either let them control us, or we can choose to control them.

It's about focusing on what we can do, rather than what we can't. It's about taking action, even when it's scary or uncomfortable. It's about believing in ourselves and our ability to create the life we desire.

In the words of the Stoic philosopher Epictetus, "The chief task in life is simply this: to identify and separate matters so that I can say clearly to myself which are externals not under my control, and which have to do with the choices I actually control."

By embracing this philosophy, by focusing on the controllables, we can navigate the challenges of life with grace, resilience, and unwavering determination. We can create a life that is truly our own, a life that is filled with joy, purpose, and meaning.

Learning from biblical stories and spiritual principles.

In my darkest hours, when the weight of the world seemed unbearable, I found guidance in the timeless wisdom of the Bible. The stories of struggle, resilience, and redemption resonated with me on a deep level, offering a roadmap for navigating my own challenges and finding meaning in my suffering.

One story that particularly resonated with me was that of Adam and Eve in the Garden of Eden. It's a story that has been told and retold for centuries, but for me, it took on a new meaning as I grappled with my own feelings of lack and scarcity.

In the biblical account, God tells Adam and Eve that they can eat freely from any tree in the garden except one. But Satan, the serpent, tempts Eve with the forbidden fruit, planting the thought of doubt and discontent in her mind. He focuses her attention on the one thing she cannot have, rather than the abundance that surrounds her. God used abundance words when it came to the garden "every, freely, and any" where they were in a place of protection & provision, yet Satan knew if he could distract them with lack, get them away from God or even have them think they were Gods.

Then it will destroy our destiny.

This, I realized, is the essence of the scarcity mindset – the belief that there is not enough to go around, that we must constantly compete and strive for limited resources or even worse, that we know everything. It's a mindset that breeds fear, anxiety, and a sense of lack.

Another biblical story that spoke to me was that of Job, a man who endured unimaginable suffering and loss. Job lost his wealth, his health, and his children, yet he remained faithful to God. In the end, God restored Job's fortunes and blessed him with even more than he had before.

Job's story taught me the importance of perseverance and faith in the face of adversity. It showed me that even when everything seems lost, there is always

hope for restoration and renewal. It reminded me that God's plans for us are often beyond our comprehension, but that we can trust in His goodness and faithfulness walking in His ways.

Lastly, one of my personal favorites is Joseph, whose story is one of incredible resilience and faith in the face of immense hardship. Joseph, the son of Jacob and Rachel, was favored by his father, which caused jealousy and resentment among his brothers. This envy led them to sell Joseph into slavery, and he was taken to Egypt. Despite his dire circumstances, Joseph remained steadfast and rose to a position of trust in the household of Potiphar, a high-ranking Egyptian official.

However, he faced another setback when Potiphar's wife falsely accused him of attempting to assault her, resulting in Joseph's imprisonment. In prison, Joseph's ability to interpret dreams came to the attention of Pharaoh, who had been troubled by perplexing dreams that none of his advisors could explain. Joseph correctly interpreted Pharaoh's dreams as a warning of seven years of plenty followed by seven years of famine. Impressed by Joseph's wisdom, Pharaoh appointed him as the governor of Egypt, placing him in charge of managing the country's resources.

Under Joseph's leadership, Egypt successfully navigated the years of famine, becoming a crucial supplier of grain to surrounding nations. When his brothers came to Egypt seeking food, Joseph forgave them and revealed his identity, demonstrating a remarkable capacity for compassion and reconciliation.

Joseph's story is a powerful example of how faith, integrity, and perseverance can lead to triumph over adversity. His journey from betrayal and slavery to becoming a key leader in Egypt highlights the profound impact of resilience and the ability to transform suffering into opportunity for the greater good.

The Bible is filled with stories of ordinary people who achieved extraordinary things through wisdom, principles, faith and perseverance. These stories offer valuable lessons about the importance of trusting in God, following His commandments, and living a life of purpose and meaning.

But the Bible is more than just a collection of stories; it's a guidebook for life, a source of wisdom and inspiration that can help us navigate the challenges and opportunities that come our way.

The principles found in the Bible, such as love, kingdom building, strength, compassion, and personal excellence, are not religious concepts; they are universal truths that can help us live happier, healthier, and more fulfilling lives.

By incorporating these principles into our daily lives, we can cultivate a positive mindset, build stronger relationships, and make a positive impact on the world around us. We can learn to see challenges as opportunities for growth, to forgive ourselves and others, and to live a life of purpose and meaning.

The Bible is not a book for the religious; it's a book for anyone seeking wisdom, guidance, and inspiration. It's a book that has the power to transform lives, to heal broken hearts, and to inspire us to become the highest versions of ourselves.

Developing emotional intelligence and self-awareness.

In the pursuit of mastering our minds, we often focus on intellect, logic, and reason. We strive to acquire knowledge, to analyze information, and to make rational decisions. But there's another aspect of our minds that is equally important, if not more so: our emotional intelligence.

Emotional intelligence, often referred to as EQ, is the ability to understand, use, and manage our own emotions in positive ways to achieve our goals. It's about recognizing and understanding our own feelings, as well as the feelings of others. It's about being able to manage our emotions effectively, to communicate clearly, to build strong relationships, and to navigate social situations with grace and empathy.

Developing emotional intelligence is a journey of self-discovery, a process of understanding our own emotional landscape and learning how to navigate it with skill and compassion. It's about recognizing our triggers, understanding our reactions, and developing healthy coping mechanisms for dealing with stress, anger, and other challenging emotions.

One of the key components of emotional intelligence is self-awareness. This involves being able to identify and understand our own emotions, to recognize how they affect our thoughts and behaviors, and to be mindful of our impact on others.

Self-awareness is not always easy. It requires us to look inward, to confront our own vulnerabilities and shortcomings. It can be uncomfortable, even painful, to acknowledge our flaws and weaknesses. But it's also incredibly liberating.

When we become self-aware, we gain a deeper understanding of ourselves and our motivations. We become more conscious of our choices and their consequences. We are better able to manage our emotions, to communicate effectively, and to build stronger relationships.

Self-awareness also allows us to identify our triggers, those situations or events that tend to evoke strong emotional reactions in us. By understanding our triggers, we can develop strategies for managing them in a healthy way.

Another important aspect of emotional intelligence is empathy, the ability to understand and share the feelings of others. Empathy allows us to connect with others on a deeper level, to build trust and rapport, and to navigate social situations with greater ease.

When we are empathetic, we are able to see the world through the eyes of others. We can understand their perspectives, their motivations, and their emotions. This allows us to communicate more effectively, to resolve conflicts peacefully, and to build stronger relationships.

Developing emotional intelligence and self-awareness is an ongoing process, one that requires patience, practice, and a willingness to learn and grow. But the rewards are immense.

When we master our emotions, we become more resilient in the face of adversity. We are better able to handle stress, overcome challenges, and bounce back from setbacks. We are also more likely to achieve our goals, to build strong relationships, and to live a life of purpose and fulfillment.

There are many resources available to help you develop your emotional intelligence and self-awareness. You can read books, attend workshops, or seek guidance from a therapist or coach. The most important thing is to be willing to do the work, to invest in yourself, and to embrace the journey of self-discovery.

Remember, emotional intelligence is not a fixed trait. It's a skill that can be learned and developed over time. With dedication and practice, you can become more self-aware, more empathetic, and more emotionally intelligent. And as you do, you'll unlock a whole new level of personal growth and fulfillment.

Mastering emotions and overcoming negative self-talk.

Our minds are powerful tools, capable of both incredible creation and devastating destruction. The thoughts we think and the words we speak to ourselves have a profound impact on our emotions, our actions, and ultimately, our lives.

For years, I allowed negative self-talk to run rampant in my mind. I told myself I wasn't good enough, smart enough, or worthy of love and success. These thoughts became a self-fulfilling prophecy, fueling my depression and anxiety, and sabotaging my efforts to create a better life.

The voice in my head was relentless, a constant critic that berated me for my mistakes, my shortcomings, and my perceived failures. It was like a dark cloud that followed me everywhere, casting a shadow over my every thought and action.

This negative self-talk was not only emotionally draining; it was also incredibly destructive. It eroded my self-confidence, fueled my fears, and prevented me from taking risks and pursuing my dreams.

I realized that if I wanted to create a better life for myself, I had to learn to master my emotions and overcome this negative self-talk. It was a daunting task, but I knew it was essential for my well-being and my future.

The first step was to become aware of my thoughts and emotions. I started paying attention to the voice in my head, noticing the patterns of negative self-talk that emerged. I also started journaling, writing down my thoughts and feelings, and exploring the root causes of my negativity.

Through this process of self-reflection, I began to understand the power of my thoughts. I realized that my thoughts were not facts, but simply interpretations of reality. I had the power to choose my thoughts, to challenge the negative ones, and to replace them with positive affirmations.

I started practicing positive self-talk, repeating affirmations like "I am worthy," "I am capable," and simply "that's not true" At first, it felt awkward and forced, but over time, these affirmations began to sink in, replacing the negative self-talk that had plagued me for so long.

I also learned to challenge my negative thoughts. When a negative thought arose, I would ask myself, "Is this thought true? Is it helpful? Is it serving me?" If the answer was no, I would consciously choose to let it go and replace it with a more positive and empowering thought.

Another powerful tool I discovered was mindfulness. By focusing on the present moment, I was able to quiet the chatter in my mind and connect with my inner peace. I started meditating regularly, practicing deep breathing exercises, and spending time in nature.

These practices helped me to become more aware of my emotions, to observe them without judgment, and to respond to them in a healthy and constructive way. I learned that emotions are not good or bad; they are simply signals that tell us something about ourselves and our needs.

By mastering my emotions, I was able to break free from the cycle of negativity that had held me captive for so long. I was no longer a slave to my thoughts and feelings; I was the master of my own mind.

Overcoming negative self-talk is an ongoing process, one that requires constant vigilance and effort. But the rewards are immeasurable. By mastering

our emotions and cultivating a positive mindset, we can unlock our full potential, achieve our dreams, and live a life of joy, peace, and fulfillment.

Remember, you are not your thoughts. You are the observer of your thoughts, the master of your mind. You have the power to choose your thoughts, to shape your reality, and to create a life that is truly your own.

The role of visualization, affirmations, and attraction in shaping reality.

In the grand theater of life, our minds are the directors, the scriptwriters, and the actors. The thoughts we think, the images we conjure, and the words we speak are the building blocks of our reality. This isn't just some New Age philosophy; it's backed by science and rooted in ancient wisdom.

Visualization: Painting Your Dreams on the Canvas of Your Mind

Visualization is the art of creating a mental picture of what you want to achieve. It's about seeing yourself already in possession of your desires, feeling the emotions associated with success, and embodying the person you need to become to reach your goals.

When I was struggling with depression and addiction, visualization was a lifeline. I would close my eyes and imagine myself healthy, happy, and successful. I would see myself running a thriving business, speaking to large audiences, and making a positive impact on the world.

These visualizations weren't just fleeting daydreams; they were vivid, detailed, and emotionally charged. I would feel the joy of accomplishment, the satisfaction of helping others, and the peace that comes with living a life of purpose.

The more I visualized, the more real my dreams became. They were no longer just abstract ideas; they were tangible goals that I could see, feel, and hear. This shift in perspective gave me the motivation and the courage to take action.

Affirmations: Speaking Your Dreams into Existence

Affirmations are positive statements that you repeat to yourself to challenge negative thoughts and reinforce positive beliefs. They are like mantras, powerful words that can reprogram your subconscious mind and shape your reality.

During my journey, throughout the day I am reciting affirmations like "I am successful," "I am a king," and "I am a leader." These simple statements, repeated with conviction, began to chip away at the layers of self-doubt and negativity that had accumulated over the years.

Affirmations are not about denying reality or pretending that everything is perfect. They are about choosing to focus on the positive, to believe in yourself and your abilities, and to speak your dreams into existence.

Attraction: Aligning Your Energy with Your Desires

The law of attraction is a powerful principle that states that we attract into our lives the things we focus on. Our thoughts, feelings, and beliefs act like magnets, drawing to us experiences and circumstances that match our dominant vibration.

When we focus on lack, we attract more lack. When we focus on fear, we attract the things we fear. But when we focus on abundance, gratitude, and joy, we open ourselves up to a world of possibilities.

I learned to harness the power of attraction by cultivating a positive mindset, practicing gratitude, and focusing on my goals. I surrounded myself with positive people, read inspiring books, and listened to podcasts of people that were where I wanted to be in life. I made a conscious effort to raise my vibration and align my energy with my desires.

The results were astounding. Opportunities began to appear out of nowhere. People who could help me achieve my goals seemed to magically enter my life. My business was beginning to grow, my relationships improved, and my overall well-being soared.

The Power of the Mind

Visualization, affirmations, and attraction are powerful tools that can help you shape your reality. They are not magic bullets, but they are effective techniques that can help you overcome obstacles, achieve your goals, and create a life you love.

The key is to use them consistently and with intention. Make visualization a daily practice. Repeat your affirmations with conviction. Focus on the positive and cultivate a mindset of gratitude.

Remember, your mind is a powerful tool. Use it wisely, and you can create a life that is beyond your wildest dreams.

Reprogramming the subconscious mind for positive change.

Our subconscious mind, a vast reservoir of beliefs, memories, and emotions, plays a pivotal role in shaping our thoughts, feelings, and actions. It's like the operating system of our mind, running in the background and influencing our behavior in ways we may not even be aware of.

For much of my life, my subconscious mind was programmed with negative beliefs and self-limiting thoughts. These deeply ingrained patterns stemmed from childhood experiences, societal conditioning, and the accumulation of past traumas. They were like invisible chains, holding me back from reaching my full potential.

But as I delved deeper into the world of personal development, I discovered that the subconscious mind is not fixed or immutable. It can be reprogrammed, rewired, and transformed. This realization was a game-changer, a beacon of hope in the midst of my despair.

Reprogramming the subconscious mind is not an overnight process; it requires patience, persistence, and a willingness to confront our deepest fears and insecurities. But the rewards are immeasurable. By changing our subconscious programming, we can transform our lives from the inside out.

One of the most effective ways to reprogram the subconscious mind is through repetition and affirmation. By repeatedly exposing ourselves to positive messages and affirmations, we can gradually overwrite the negative programming that has been holding us back.

This is where the power of visualization and affirmations comes into play. By visualizing ourselves achieving our goals and repeating positive affirmations about ourselves and our lives, we can create new neural pathways in our brains, reinforcing positive beliefs and behaviors.

Another powerful tool for reprogramming the subconscious mind is doing what you say you are going to do. You must keep your word with yourself. Everytime you tell yourself you're going to eat healthy, stop drinking, go to the gym, and don't do it. Your subconscious mind remembers this deteriorating your confidence with self doubt, but when you follow through with every action it strengthens your confidence subconsciously.

Meditation and mindfulness practices can also be effective in reprogramming the subconscious mind. By cultivating present-moment awareness and observing our thoughts and feelings without judgment, we can gain insights into our subconscious programming and begin to make conscious choices about the thoughts and beliefs we want to cultivate.

In addition to these techniques, it's important to surround ourselves with positive influences and to create a supportive environment that reinforces our desired changes. This may involve spending time with positive people, reading uplifting books, listening to motivational podcasts, and engaging in activities that raise your vibration bringing us joy and fulfillment.

Reprogramming the subconscious mind is a journey of self-discovery and transformation. It's about shedding old, limiting beliefs and embracing new, empowering ones. It's about rewiring our brains for success, happiness, and abundance.

As I embarked on this journey, I discovered that the subconscious mind is not just a storehouse of memories and emotions; it's a powerful ally in our quest for personal growth and transformation. By learning to harness its power, we can unlock our full potential and create a life that is truly extraordinary.

The process of reprogramming my subconscious mind is not always easy. There are times when old patterns and beliefs resurfaced, threatening to derail my progress. But I persevered, drawing strength from my faith, my support system, and my unwavering commitment to change.

Through repetition, affirmation, visualization, meditation, and mindfulness, I gradually rewired my subconscious mind for positive change. I replaced self-doubt with self-belief, fear with courage, and scarcity with abundance.

The transformation was remarkable. I felt lighter, happier, and more confident. I started attracting positive opportunities into my life, my relationships improved, and my business began to thrive.

Reprogramming my subconscious mind was one of the most empowering experiences of my life. It taught me that I am not a victim of my past, but a co-creator of my future. It showed me that I have the power to change my thoughts, my beliefs, and my reality.

Cultivating resilience and mental toughness.

Life is a series of peaks and valleys, triumphs and setbacks. It's not about avoiding the valleys, but about learning to navigate them with grace and resilience. Mental toughness isn't about being invincible; it's about embracing the challenges, learning from them, and emerging stronger on the other side.

My journey has been far from easy. I've faced financial hardships, racial prejudice, devastating losses, and the crippling weight of depression. But through it all, I've discovered that resilience is not a trait we're born with; it's a muscle we build through facing adversity.

So, how do we cultivate this resilience, this mental toughness that allows us to weather life's storms? It starts with a shift in mindset.

1. **Embrace the Struggle:** Challenges are not roadblocks; they're detours on the path to growth. Each obstacle we overcome, each setback we face, is an opportunity to learn, to adapt, and to become stronger. As the saying goes, "Smooth seas do not make skillful sailors."

2. **Reframe Your Perspective:** Our thoughts shape our reality. When faced with adversity, it's easy to fall into a spiral of negativity and self-doubt. But by consciously choosing to reframe our perspective, we can find the silver lining in every cloud. Instead of asking, "Why me?" ask, "What can I learn from this?"

3. **Practice Gratitude:** Gratitude is a powerful antidote to negativity. When we focus on what we have, rather than what we lack, we shift our energy and attract more abundance into our lives. Take time each day to reflect on the things you're grateful for, no matter how small they may seem.

4. **Build a Support System:** You don't have to go through life's challenges alone. Surround yourself with positive, supportive people who believe in you and your dreams.

Lean on your friends, family, mentors, or a therapist when you need to. Remember, it's okay to ask for help.

5. **Take Care of Your Physical Health:** Your mental and physical health are interconnected. Regular exercise, a healthy diet, and adequate sleep are essential for maintaining emotional well-being and resilience. When you feel good physically, you're better equipped to handle stress and adversity.

6. **Develop Positive Coping Mechanisms:** Everyone has different ways of coping with stress and adversity. Some people find solace in meditation or prayer, while others turn to exercise, creative pursuits, or spending time in nature. Find what works for you and make it a regular part of your routine.

7. **Set Realistic Goals:** Setting achievable goals and celebrating small victories can boost your confidence and resilience. Have one main goal broken down into smaller, more manageable steps, and track your progress along the way.

8. **Learn from Your Mistakes:** Mistakes are inevitable, but they don't have to define you. Instead of dwelling on your failures, view them as learning opportunities. Analyze what went wrong, take responsibility for your actions, and use the experience to grow and improve.

9. **Practice Self-Compassion:** Be kind to yourself, especially during difficult times. We all make mistakes, we all have setbacks, and we all experience pain. Don't beat yourself

up for not being perfect. Instead, offer yourself the same compassion and understanding you would offer a friend.

The importance of seeking guidance and mentorship.

In the depths of my despair, as I teetered on the precipice of self-destruction, I realized that I couldn't do it alone. I had exhausted my own resources, my own willpower, my own understanding. I needed help, guidance, a lifeline to pull me back from the brink.

It was then that I turned to mentors, individuals who had walked a similar path, who had faced their own demons and emerged victorious. They were beacons of hope in my darkest hour, offering wisdom, support, and a roadmap to recovery.

One of my mentors Augustine always says "Stop trying to figure it out, and just follow direction."

Through the guidance of my mentors, I began to see that the path has already been laid out before me. I saw my life in a new light. I realized that I was not alone, that I was part of something bigger than myself, and that I had a purpose to fulfill in this world.

The impact of mentorship on my life was profound. My mentors provided me with the support, guidance, tools and real world experience I needed to overcome my depression, learn skills and rebuild my life. They helped me to develop a stronger sense of self, a clearer understanding of my purpose, and a more positive outlook on life.

But the benefits of mentorship extend far beyond personal growth. Mentors can also provide valuable career advice, networking opportunities, and access to resources that can help you achieve your goals.

Research has shown that mentorship can have a significant impact on career success. A study found that employees who had mentors were promoted five times more often than those who did not have mentors. Another study by the Harvard Business Review found that mentees were more likely to receive raises and promotions, and to be satisfied with their jobs.

Mentorship is not just for young people starting out in their careers. It can be beneficial at any stage of life. Whether you're a student, a professional, or an entrepreneur, having a mentor can help you to navigate challenges, make better decisions, and achieve your goals.

If you're considering seeking guidance from a mentor, there are a few things to keep in mind. First, it's important to find someone who you respect and admire, someone who has achieved the kind of success you aspire to.

Second, be clear about your goals and what you hope to gain from the mentorship relationship. This will help your mentor to tailor their guidance to your specific needs.

Finally, honor and serve be sure to add value not being the type to take take take. You also need to be a student, open to feedback and willing to learn.

Mentorship is a two-way street, and you'll get the most out of it if you're actively engaged in the process.

Seeking guidance and mentorship was a turning point in my life. It helped me to overcome adversity, to find my purpose, and to create a life that is filled with meaning, and fulfillment. I am eternally grateful to my mentors for their wisdom, support, and unwavering belief in me.

CHAPTER 3

BIG RISK, BIG REWARD

Let's get it my friends, this chapter is where things get really interesting. We're about to dive headfirst into the sometimes terrifying, but always rewarding world of risk-taking.

Now, before you start picturing me base jumping off skyscrapers or betting my life savings on a roulette wheel, let's get one thing straight: risk doesn't always have to be synonymous with recklessness. In fact, the most successful risk-takers are those who approach it with a calculated mindset, a clear vision, and a healthy dose of courage.

I've always been a bit of a risk-taker myself. From starting my own business at 18 to speaking my truth in the face of adversity, I've never shied away from stepping outside my comfort zone. And let me tell you, it hasn't always been easy. I've faced my fair share of setbacks, failures, and moments of self-doubt.

But I've also learned that the greatest rewards in life often come from taking the biggest risks. Whether it's starting a new venture, pursuing a passion, or simply speaking the truth, stepping into the unknown can lead to incredible growth, fulfillment, and opportunities you never thought possible.

In this chapter, we'll explore the art and science of risk-taking. We'll delve into the psychology behind fear and uncertainty, and discover how to overcome these obstacles to unlock our full potential. We'll examine the strategies that successful risk-takers use to assess and mitigate risk, and we'll learn how to embrace failure as a stepping stone to success.

I'll share personal stories from my own life, highlighting the times I've taken big risks and the lessons I've learned along the way. We'll also look at inspiring examples of individuals who achieved greatness by daring to step outside the box and challenge the status quo.

But most importantly, I hope this chapter empowers you to take your own leap of faith. To embrace the unknown, to chase your dreams, and to create a life that is truly extraordinary. Because at the end of the day, the biggest risk you can take is not taking any risk at all.

So, are you ready to step up your game and embrace the power of risk? Let's dive in and discover the incredible rewards that await you on the other side of fear.

The importance of taking calculated risks for growth.

Life is a series of choices, a constant dance between the familiar and the unknown. We can choose to play it safe, to stay within the confines of our comfort zones, or we can choose to embrace the thrill of the unknown, to step outside the lines and take a risk.

Risk, often perceived as a gamble, a leap of faith into the uncertain, is in fact, the catalyst for growth. It's the spark that ignites our potential, the force that propels us beyond our perceived limitations. Without risk, we stagnate, we wither, we become a shadow of what we could be.

Taking risks doesn't mean blindly jumping into the abyss. It's about calculated decisions, informed choices that are aligned with our values, goals, and aspirations. It's about weighing the potential rewards against the potential risks, and having the courage to move forward even when the outcome is uncertain.

In my own life, I've taken countless risks, some small, some monumental. Each one has taught me valuable lessons, shaped my character, and propelled me towards growth.

One of the biggest risks I took was starting my own business. I had no business knowledge, no business plan, just a burning passion for art, custom sneakers and taking care of my family. I invested my time, my energy, and all my earnings into this venture, unsure of whether it would succeed or fail.

The early days were filled with uncertainty and self-doubt. I questioned my abilities, my decisions, my sanity. There were sleepless nights, countless setbacks, and moments when I wanted to throw in the towel.

But I persevered. I learned from my mistakes, adapted to the challenges, and kept pushing forward. And slowly but surely, my business began to thrive. I started receiving orders from all over the country, my social media following grew, and I was able to turn my passion into a profitable venture.

The rewards of taking that risk were immense. Not only did I achieve financial independence, but I also gained a sense of purpose and fulfillment that I had never experienced before. I discovered my entrepreneurial spirit, my ability to create something from nothing, and my passion for helping others express their individuality through their footwear.

But the rewards of risk-taking go beyond the material. Taking risks forces us to step outside our comfort zones, to confront our fears, and to discover hidden strengths and talents we never knew we had. It expands our horizons, broadens our perspectives, and opens us up to new possibilities.

Risk-taking is not just about achieving external success; it's about personal growth and transformation. It's about becoming the best version of ourselves, about living a life that is bold, adventurous, and fulfilling.

Of course, not all risks lead to success. There will be setbacks, failures, and disappointments along the way. But even in failure, there is value. Failure is not the opposite of success; it's a stepping stone on the path to success. It's an opportunity to learn, to grow, and to come back stronger.

The key is to learn from our mistakes, to adapt our strategies, and to never give up on our dreams. As the saying goes, "The only real failure in life is the failure to try."

So, I encourage you to embrace the power of risk-taking. Don't let fear hold you back. Step outside your comfort zone, pursue your passions, and chase your dreams. The rewards may not always be immediate or obvious, but the personal growth and transformation that come from taking risks are invaluable.

Remember, life is too short to play it safe. Take a chance, embrace the unknown, and see where the journey takes you. You might be surprised at what you discover about yourself and the world around you.

Personal stories of taking big risks and the lessons learned.

Life is a series of choices, a constant dance between playing it safe and taking a leap of faith. I've always been one to embrace the unknown, to chase after my dreams with reckless abandon, even when the odds were stacked against me. This chapter is dedicated to those moments of daring, those times when I threw caution to the wind and embraced the exhilarating, terrifying, world of risk-taking.

One of my earliest leaps into risk-taking was my decision to pursue a career in art and custom sneakers. Fresh out of high school, with my football dreams dashed by injuries, I found myself at a crossroads. I could have chosen the safe route, gotten a traditional job, and settled into a comfortable but unfulfilling life. But something inside me yearned for more.

I had discovered a passion for art, a love for transforming ordinary sneakers into unique works of art. It was a risky path, one that offered no guarantees of success. But I knew that if I didn't take the leap, I would always regret it.

So, I took a chance. I invested my money in art supplies, set up a makeshift studio in my bedroom, and started creating. I spent countless hours honing my skills, experimenting with different techniques, and developing my own unique style.

Taking risks has always been a part of my journey, and my experiences have taught me invaluable lessons. I remember this one time in my high school days when I was about 16 or 17 years old. I had my own clothing brand called The Real See Fake, which had started gaining traction. I planned a significant winter drop, creating a buzz and generating excitement. The collection included hoodies, beanies, long-sleeved t-shirts, sweatpants, and sweat suits with super dope designs. Previously, a t-shirt and long-sleeved drop had gone

well, so I felt confident. I decided to work with a young local vinyl printer, a fellow young hustler, introduced to me by a good friend who was also a business owner. We built a great relationship, and I trusted him with this large order, seeing it as an excellent opportunity for both of us.

However, I didn't have the full investment amount, so I borrowed around $3,000 from a friend, putting all my money and trust into this venture. Instead of a partial deposit, I handed over the full amount in cash, eager to see my designs come to life. Unfortunately, communication with the printer became inconsistent, and after weeks and months of excuses, he delivered a box of poorly made products. Logos were upside down, peeling, and embroidery was incomplete, representing only about 15% of my order. I never got my money back or heard from him again, a harsh lesson in trust and business practices.

A year or so later, having gained some experience and growing my custom sneaker brand, I decided to invest significantly in a new sneaker project. Inspired by a recent release by this popular brand I'm not going to mention, I envisioned a vibrant collection with unique colorways. I ordered around 100 pairs of them in all white (again brand I'm not going to mention), investing five to six figures into sneakers, materials and equipment. Starting with six pairs in various colors, I decided to focus on the most promising ones— blue, purple, pink, and yellow. The yellow ones were particularly popular, and I had high hopes for this collection. However, just as the orders started rolling in, Puma discontinued the silhouette, cutting off my supply. Despite scouring every possible source, I couldn't fulfill my orders. To make matters worse, a few months later, This brand released two colorways strikingly similar to my designs. In this situation, I lost close to six figures, a significant financial blow.

These experiences taught me the importance of careful planning, prudent financial management, and the unpredictability of business ventures. Taking risks is essential for growth, but it also involves setbacks and disappointments. Nonetheless, these lessons have been crucial in shaping my approach to business and life.

I faced countless challenges and lost friends along the way. There were times when I doubted my abilities, when I questioned my decision to pursue such an unconventional path. There were financial struggles, creative blocks, and moments of sheer exhaustion.

But I persevered. I pushed through the self-doubt, the fear of failure, and the naysayers who told me I was wasting my time. I fueled my passion with unwavering determination, fueled by the belief that I was meant for something more.

And slowly but surely, my hard work began to pay off. My custom sneakers started gaining attention, first from friends and family, then from a wider audience on social media. Orders started coming in, and I found myself working day and night to keep up with the demand.

The thrill of seeing my creations come to life, of knowing that I was making a living doing something I loved, was indescribable. It was a validation of my risk, a testament to the power of following your heart and pursuing your passions.

But my journey as an entrepreneur was far from over. In fact, it was just beginning. I faced numerous setbacks and challenges along the way, from financial struggles to creative blocks to the ever-present fear of failure.

One of the biggest risks I took was moving to Charlotte, North Carolina, to expand my business and start a new life with my girlfriend. It was a bold move, one that required me to step outside of my comfort zone and embrace the unknown.

The move was initially successful. My business thrived, I connected with a vibrant community of artists and creatives, and I was building a life that I loved. But then, disaster struck. A fire in our apartment complex destroyed almost everything we owned, leaving us homeless and financially devastated.

It was a devastating blow, one that tested my resilience and my faith in myself. I could have easily given up, returned home, and abandoned my dreams. But I refused to let this setback define me.

Instead, I used it as an opportunity to learn and grow. I reevaluated my priorities, strengthened my resolve, and doubled down on my commitment to my business and my family. I learned the importance of mitigating risk, of diversifying my income streams, and of always being prepared for the unexpected.

The fire was a painful experience, but it also taught me valuable lessons about resilience, adaptability, and the importance of never giving up on your dreams. It showed me that even in the face of adversity, there is always a way forward, always a chance to rise from the ashes and create a better future.

These are just a few of the many risks I've taken in my life. Some have paid off handsomely, while others have resulted in setbacks and disappointments. But through it all, I've learned that taking risks is an essential part of growth, of pushing boundaries, and of discovering what we're truly capable of.

The lessons I've learned from risk-taking have been invaluable. They've taught me the importance of preparation, the power of perseverance, and the value of learning from my mistakes. They've shown me that even the biggest

failures can be stepping stones to success, and that the greatest rewards often come from taking the biggest risks.

Assessing risk and reward before making major decisions.

Life is a series of choices, each one a fork in the road leading to different destinations. Some choices are small and inconsequential, while others have the power to alter the course of our lives. These major decisions, whether they involve starting a business, changing careers, making the move or investing in a relationship, often come with a hefty dose of risk and uncertainty.

The fear of the unknown can be paralyzing, holding us back from taking the leap and pursuing our dreams. But what if we could approach these decisions with a sense of clarity and confidence? What if we could assess the risks and rewards involved, weigh the potential outcomes, and make informed choices that align with our values and goals?

That's where the art of risk assessment comes in. It's not about eliminating risk altogether; that's impossible. It's about understanding the risks involved, mitigating them where possible, and making calculated decisions that have the potential to yield significant rewards.

In my own life, I've faced numerous major decisions, each one fraught with risk and uncertainty. When I decided to start my custom sneaker business, I had no guarantee of success. I was investing my time, money, and energy into a venture that could easily fail. But I also saw the potential for great reward – the opportunity to turn my passion into a profitable business, to express my creativity, and to make a positive impact on the world.

Before taking the leap, I spent time researching the market, analyzing my competition, and developing a business plan. I talked to other entrepreneurs, sought advice from mentors, and weighed the potential risks and rewards.

I knew that there was a chance I could fail, that I could lose everything I had invested. But I also knew that if I didn't take the risk, I would always wonder what could have been. I would always regret not having the courage to pursue my dreams.

So, I took the leap. I invested my savings, didn't go to college, and poured my heart and soul into my business. It was a gamble, but it was a calculated one. I had done my research, assessed the risks, developed a plan to mitigate them and most importantly put the work in!

The business didn't take off overnight. There were setbacks, challenges, and moments of doubt. But I persevered, learning from my mistakes, adapting to the market, and constantly striving to improve.

And eventually, my hard work paid off. The business started to grow, my customer base expanded, and I began to see a return on my investment. The rewards were not just financial; they were also emotional and psychological. I felt a sense of accomplishment, honor, and fulfillment that I had never experienced before.

The decision to move to Charlotte was another major risk I took. I was leaving behind the familiar comforts of home, the support system of my family and friends, and the only life I had ever known. But I was also drawn to the city's vibrant energy, its growing art scene, and the opportunity to build a new life with the woman I loved.

Before making the move, I weighed the potential risks and rewards. I knew that there was a chance I could struggle financially, that I could feel isolated

and alone, that the relationship might not work out. But I also saw the potential for great reward – the opportunity to pursue my dreams, to experience a new culture, and to build a life filled with love and adventure.

The move to Charlotte was a rollercoaster ride of emotions. There were moments of joy, excitement, and wonder, as I explored the city and connected with new people. But there were also moments of loneliness, frustration, and despair, as I struggled to find my footing and adapt to a new environment.

The fire in our apartment complex was a major setback, one that tested our resilience and our commitment to each other. But it also brought us closer together, forcing us to rely on each other for support and to re-evaluate our priorities.

In the end, the move to Charlotte was a valuable learning experience. It taught me the importance of adaptability, resilience, and the willingness to embrace change. It showed me that even when things don't go according to plan, there is always an opportunity for growth and transformation.

Assessing risk and reward before making major decisions is a crucial skill for anyone who wants to live a life of purpose and fulfillment. It's not about avoiding risk; it's about understanding the risks involved, mitigating them where possible, and making informed choices that align with your values and goals.

By taking calculated risks, we open ourselves up to new opportunities, new experiences, and new possibilities. We learn, we grow, and we evolve. We become the best versions of ourselves.

Overcoming fear and uncertainty associated with risk-taking.

Let's face it: taking risks is scary. It's stepping into the unknown, venturing outside our comfort zones, and facing the possibility of failure. The fear and uncertainty that accompany risk-taking can be paralyzing, holding us back from pursuing our dreams and reaching our full potential.

I know this fear all too well. When I first started my custom sneaker business, I was terrified. I had no formal training, no business plan, and no guarantee of success. I was putting myself out there, risking my time, my money, and my reputation.

The fear of failure was a constant companion, whispering doubts in my ear and casting shadows on my dreams. What if no one liked my designs? What if I couldn't make enough money to support myself? What if I failed miserably and became a laughingstock?

These fears were not unfounded. The entrepreneurial world is littered with stories of failed businesses, broken dreams, and financial ruin. The statistics are sobering: according to the Small

Business Administration, only about half of all new businesses survive five years.

But I also knew that without risk, there could be no reward. I had seen firsthand the transformative power of taking chances, of stepping outside my comfort zone, and of pursuing my passions with unwavering determination.

So, how did I overcome the fear and uncertainty that threatened to hold me back? It wasn't easy, but I developed a few strategies that helped me to face my fears head-on and embrace the risks that came with pursuing my dreams.

1. **Acknowledge Your Fears:** The first step to overcoming fear is to acknowledge it. Don't try to suppress it or pretend it doesn't exist. Instead, face it head-on. What are you afraid of? What are the worst-case scenarios? Once you've identified your fears, you can start to address them.

2. **Challenge Your Assumptions:** Often, our fears are based on assumptions and beliefs that may not be entirely accurate. Challenge those assumptions. Are they based on facts or on irrational fears? Are they holding you back from taking action? By questioning your assumptions, you can start to reframe your thinking and see the situation in a new light.

3. **Focus on the Positives:** Instead of dwelling on the potential negatives, focus on the potential positives. What could you gain by taking this risk? What are the potential rewards? Visualize yourself achieving your goals and experiencing the success you desire.

4. **Take Small Steps:** You don't have to take a giant leap of faith all at once. Start by taking small, manageable steps towards your goal. Each step you take will build your confidence and make the next step easier.

5. **Build a Support System:** Surround yourself with people who believe in you and your dreams. Seek out mentors, coaches, or friends who can offer guidance, encouragement, and support.

6. **Embrace Failure as a Learning Opportunity:** Failure is not the end; it's a stepping stone to success. Every successful entrepreneur has experienced setbacks and failures along the way. The key is to learn from your mistakes, adjust your approach, and keep moving forward.

7. **Trust Your Intuition:** Your gut feeling is often a good indicator of whether or not a risk is worth taking. Listen to your intuition, but also do your research and gather as much information as possible before making a decision.

Overcoming fear and uncertainty is an ongoing process. There will always be new challenges and risks to face. But by developing these strategies and cultivating a mindset of resilience and determination, you can learn to embrace the unknown and pursue your dreams with confidence.

Remember, the greatest risk is not taking one at all. By playing it safe, you may avoid failure, but you also miss out on the opportunity for growth, success, and fulfillment. So, take a deep breath, step outside your comfort zone, and embrace the adventure that awaits you. The rewards may be greater than you ever imagined.

The role of preparation and planning in mitigating risks.

Taking risks is like embarking on a thrilling adventure. It's about stepping into the unknown, pushing your boundaries, and chasing after your dreams. But just like any adventure, it's important to be prepared. You wouldn't climb Mount Everest without proper gear and training, would you? The same principle applies to taking risks in life.

Preparation and planning are the unsung heroes of risk mitigation. They are the compass that guides you through the uncharted waters of uncertainty, the safety net that catches you when you stumble, and the toolkit that equips you to overcome challenges.

Think of it this way: every risk you take is like a seed you plant. Preparation and planning are the fertile soil, the sunlight, and the water that nourish that seed and help it grow into a thriving plant. Without them, the seed may never germinate, or it may wither and die before it reaches its full potential.

In my own entrepreneurial journey, I've learned firsthand the importance of preparation and planning. When I first started my custom sneaker business, I was so eager to get started that I jumped in headfirst without a clear plan. I made mistakes, lost money, lots of money, and faced numerous setbacks.

But I learned from those mistakes. I realized that taking risks without a solid plan was like driving a car without a GPS. You might get lucky and end up where you want to go, but chances are, you'll get lost and lose time.

So, I started to educate myself. I read books, attended seminars, and sought advice from mentors. I learned about marketing, personal development, financial management, customer service, and all the other aspects of running a successful business.

I also started to develop a plan. I set clear goals, outlined my strategies, and created a timeline for achieving my objectives. I identified potential risks and developed contingency plans to address them.

The more I prepared and planned, the more confident I became in my ability to take risks and succeed. I realized that preparation and planning weren't about eliminating risk altogether; they were about managing it, about minimizing the potential downside and maximizing the potential upside.

Preparation and planning also helped me to overcome the fear and uncertainty that often accompany risk-taking. When you have a clear plan and you've done your homework, you're less likely to be paralyzed by fear. You know what you need to do, and you have the confidence to take action.

Of course, even the best-laid plans can go awry. There will always be unforeseen challenges and unexpected setbacks. But when you're prepared, you're better equipped to handle those challenges and adapt to changing circumstances.

Preparation and planning are not just about mitigating risks; they're also about seizing opportunities. When you're prepared, you're more likely to recognize and capitalize on opportunities that come your way. You're able to act quickly and decisively, without hesitation or second-guessing.

In the words of King Solomon, known for his wisdom, emphasized the importance of preparation in several of his proverbs. One of the notable references is from Proverbs 6:6-8, where he advises people to consider the ant's ways and be wise: "Go to the ant, you sluggard; consider its ways and be wise! It has no commander, no overseer or ruler, yet it stores its provisions in summer and gathers its food at harvest." This passage highlights the value of foresight, diligence, and preparing ahead of time to ensure one's needs are met in the future. Solomon's wisdom often revolved around practical advice for living a prudent and successful life, and preparation is a recurring theme in his teachings. This quote perfectly encapsulates the importance of preparation and planning in any endeavor, especially when it comes to taking risks.

So, if you're considering taking a risk, whether it's starting a new passion, pursuing a new career, or moving to a new city, take the time to prepare and plan. Do your research, set clear goals, and develop a solid strategy. Identify potential risks and develop contingency plans.

Remember, preparation and planning are not a guarantee of success, but they significantly increase your chances of achieving your goals. They give you the confidence, the knowledge, and the tools you need to navigate the uncertain waters of risk-taking and emerge victorious.

So, go ahead and take that leap of faith. But before you do, make sure you're prepared. Because in the world of risk-taking, preparation and planning are your best allies.

Embracing failure as a learning opportunity.

In the pursuit of big rewards, it's inevitable to encounter setbacks and failures. The path to success is rarely a straight line; it's often a winding road filled with unexpected detours and roadblocks. But what separates those who ultimately achieve their goals from those who don't is their ability to embrace failure as a learning opportunity.

I've had my fair share of failures, both in my personal and professional life. I've launched businesses that flopped, invested in projects that tanked, and made decisions that I later regretted. There have been times when I felt like a complete failure, like I was never going to amount to anything.

But through it all, I've learned that failure is not the end of the road; it's simply a detour. It's a chance to learn, to grow, and to come back stronger than ever before.

One of my biggest failures was my first attempt at entrepreneurship. I had poured my heart and soul into my custom sneaker business, but it ultimately failed due to a combination of factors, including poor financial management, lack of marketing, and unrealistic expectations.

The failure of my business was a crushing blow. I felt like I had let myself and my loved ones down. I was ashamed, embarrassed, and filled with self-doubt. I questioned my abilities, my judgment, and my worth as an entrepreneur.

But as I wallowed in my self-pity, I realized that I was missing a crucial opportunity. Instead of dwelling on my failures, I could use them as a learning experience. I could analyze what went wrong, identify my mistakes, and use that knowledge to improve my future endeavors.

So, I picked myself up, dusted myself off, and started again. I took the lessons I had learned from my failed businesses and applied them to my next venture. I am more careful with my finances, more strategic with my marketing, and more realistic with my expectations.

And while my next venture hasn't made me a millionaire yet, it has been a success in its own right. It taught me valuable lessons about perseverance, resilience, and the importance of learning from my mistakes.

I've come to realize that failure is not something to be feared, but rather something to be embraced. It's a natural part of the learning process, a stepping stone on the path to success.

As the author and motivational speaker John C. Maxwell once said, "Fail early, fail often, but always fail forward."

Failing forward means using your failures as fuel for growth. It means analyzing your mistakes, learning from them, and using that knowledge to improve your future endeavors. It means not letting your failures define you, but rather using them as a springboard to success.

Embracing failure as a learning opportunity requires a shift in mindset. It means letting go of the fear of failure and embracing the unknown. It means being willing to take risks, to step outside of your comfort zone, and to learn from your mistakes.

It also means having the courage to try again, even when you've been knocked down. It means getting back up, dusting yourself off, and continuing on your journey with renewed determination.

Remember, every successful person has failed at some point in their life. The difference is that they didn't let their failures define them. They used their failures as fuel for growth, as a stepping stone to success.

So, the next time you face a setback or failure, don't despair. Embrace it as a learning opportunity. Analyze what went wrong, learn from your mistakes, and use that knowledge to improve your future endeavors.

Remember, failure is not the opposite of success; it's part of the journey. It's a chance to learn, to grow, and to come back stronger than ever before.

Inspiring examples of individuals who achieved greatness through risk-taking.

Throughout history, countless individuals have dared to defy the odds, to step outside their comfort zones, and to embrace the unknown. Their stories are testaments to the power of risk-taking, the transformative potential of venturing into uncharted territories, and the extraordinary rewards that await those who dare to dream big. One such figure is Abraham, whose story is one of incredible faith and risk-taking in the face of the unknown.

Abraham, originally named Abram, lived in the city of Ur, in Mesopotamia. He received a divine call from God, instructing him to leave his homeland, his relatives, and his father's house to go to a land that God would show him. This call was a monumental risk, asking Abraham to leave behind everything familiar and venture into an unknown land based solely on God's promise. Despite the uncertainty, Abraham displayed unwavering faith. He obeyed God's command without hesitation, embarking on a journey to Canaan with his wife, Sarah, and his nephew, Lot. This journey was full of challenges, including famine, conflicts, and the need to navigate foreign territories. Yet, Abraham's faith in God's promises remained steadfast.

Abraham's life was marked by several significant risks. He trusted God's promise that he would become the father of a great nation, even when he and Sarah were advanced in age and childless. Later, his faith was tested further when God asked him to sacrifice his son Isaac, the child of promise. Abraham's willingness to obey, even in this heart-wrenching situation, exemplified his profound faith and trust in God. At the last moment, God intervened and provided a ram for the sacrifice, reaffirming His promises to Abraham.

Abraham's story is a powerful example of how faith, integrity, and perseverance can lead to triumph over adversity. His journey from leaving his homeland to becoming a great name and the patriarch of a great nation highlights the profound impact of resilience and the ability to transform the unknown into a pathway to greatness. Abraham's legacy teaches us that the path to extraordinary achievements is often paved with challenges that test our resolve and faith.

Another inspiring example is Steve Jobs, a visionary whose innovations have transformed multiple industries. Jobs' journey began with the founding of Apple as a college dropout in his parents' garage, where he and Steve Wozniak built the first Apple computers. This humble beginning laid the foundation for what would become one of the most influential tech companies in history.

Jobs' path was fraught with challenges. In 1985, he was ousted from Apple, the company he co-founded. However, he didn't let this setback define him. Instead, Jobs founded NeXT, a computer platform development company, and acquired Pixar, which would later revolutionize the animation industry with hits like "Toy Story."

In 1997, Jobs returned to Apple, which was struggling at the time. His return marked the beginning of a new era of innovation. Under his leadership, Apple introduced groundbreaking products such as the iMac, iPod, iPhone, and iPad. These devices not only redefined their respective markets but also set new standards for design and functionality.

Jobs faced skepticism and criticism throughout his career. His demanding nature and unconventional ideas often drew doubt and resistance. Yet, his unwavering vision and relentless pursuit of excellence propelled Apple to unprecedented heights.

Today, Apple's products have become integral to modern life, influencing how we communicate, work, and entertain ourselves. Jobs' story is a testament to the power of resilience, innovation, and the willingness to take risks. His legacy continues to inspire entrepreneurs and innovators around the world to challenge the status quo and strive for greatness.

The importance of having a support system and mentors.

In the depths of my despair, when the weight of the world felt unbearable, I discovered a lifeline that would pull me back from the brink: the unwavering support of my loved ones and the guidance of mentors who believed in me, even when I didn't believe in myself.

My family, my rock, my foundation, rallied around me during my darkest hour. My mother, with her endless love and unwavering faith, offered a shoulder to cry on and a listening ear. She reminded me of my worth, my potential, and the countless blessings in my life. My father, a man of few words but immense strength, offered quiet encouragement and unwavering support. He reminded me of the importance of perseverance, of never giving up, even when the road ahead seemed impossible.

My sisters, my first friends and confidantes, showered me with love, laughter, and tough love when I needed it most. They reminded me of the joy and beauty that still existed in the world, even when I couldn't see it myself. They challenged me to be better, to push myself, and to never lose sight of my dreams.

But it wasn't just my family who lifted me up. Friends, both old and new, reached out with words of encouragement, offers of help, and a reminder that I wasn't alone in my struggles. Their presence in my life was a beacon of hope, a testament to the power of human connection and the importance of community.

In addition to my personal support system, I also sought guidance from mentors who had walked a similar path. These were individuals who had overcome their own challenges, achieved success in their chosen fields, and were willing to share their wisdom and experience with me.

One such mentor is a successful young entrepreneur who has built a multi-million dollar business from scratch. He's teaching me the importance of knowledge, having a clear vision, a solid plan, and the resilience to overcome obstacles. He shared his own stories of failure and triumph, reminding me that setbacks are inevitable but not insurmountable.

Another mentor was a spiritual leader who helped me reconnect with my faith. He guided me through the scriptures, taught me the power of prayer and principles, and helped me to find meaning and purpose in my suffering. He reminded me that I was not alone, and that I had a divine purpose to fulfill in this world.

These mentors, with their wisdom, experience, and unwavering belief in my potential, play a pivotal role in my journey. They helped me to see myself in a new light, to recognize my strengths, and to overcome my self-doubt. They empowered me to take control of my life, to make positive changes, and to pursue my dreams with renewed vigor.

The importance of having a support system and mentors cannot be overstated. They provide us with the encouragement, guidance, and accountability we need to navigate life's challenges and achieve our goals. They remind us of our worth, our potential, and our purpose.

In the words of motivational speaker Jim Rohn, "You are the average of the five people you spend the most time with." The people we surround ourselves with have a profound impact on our thoughts, beliefs, and behaviors.

If we want to achieve success and fulfillment in life, it's essential to surround ourselves with positive, supportive people who believe in us and our dreams. We need people who will challenge us to be better, who will hold us accountable, and who will celebrate our victories with us.

Mentors, in particular, can play a crucial role in our personal and professional development. They offer guidance, wisdom, and a roadmap to success. They help us to avoid common pitfalls, to learn from their mistakes, and to accelerate our growth.

Finding a mentor can be a daunting task, but it's worth the effort. Look for someone who has achieved what you want to achieve, who embodies the qualities you admire, and who is willing to invest their time and energy in your growth. Remember some are within reach and some are not, that shouldn't stop you from learning from them.

Don't be afraid to ask for help. Most successful people are happy to share their knowledge and experience with others but honor them, and provide more value then you take. Reach out to people you admire, attend networking events, and join a community of like minded individuals. You never know where you might find your next mentor.

Remember, you are not alone on this journey. There are people who care about you, who believe in you, and who want to see you succeed. Reach out to them, lean on them, and let them be your guiding light through the darkness.

And if you're fortunate enough to find a mentor, cherish that relationship. Serve and honor them, be open to their guidance, learn from their wisdom, and express your gratitude for their support. A good mentor can change your life, and their impact will be felt for years to come.

Celebrating successes and learning from failures.

The personal development journey is a rollercoaster, filled with exhilarating highs and crushing lows. It's a path paved with both triumphs and setbacks, a constant dance between success and failure. And it's in this dance that we truly learn, grow, and evolve.

Celebrating successes is an essential part of the personal development journey. It's about acknowledging our hard work, our dedication, and our resilience. It's about recognizing the milestones we've reached, the obstacles we've overcome, and the impact we've made.

When we celebrate our successes, we reinforce our belief in ourselves and our abilities. We create a positive feedback loop that fuels our motivation and propels us forward. We also inspire others, showing them what's possible when we dare to dream big and take bold action.

But celebrating success isn't just about popping champagne and recognizing your wins. It's also about taking the time to reflect on what worked, what didn't, and what we can learn from our experiences. It's about extracting valuable lessons that we can apply to future endeavors, ensuring that our successes are not just fleeting moments but stepping stones to even greater achievements.

And what about failures? Those dreaded setbacks that can leave us feeling defeated, discouraged, and questioning our abilities. How do we deal with those?

The truth is, failure is an inevitable part of the entrepreneurial journey. No one gets it right all the time. Even the most successful entrepreneurs have faced their fair share of setbacks and disappointments.

But here's the key: it's not about avoiding failure; it's about learning from it. Failure is not the opposite of success; it's a stepping stone on the path to success.

When we fail, we have the opportunity to learn valuable lessons, to gain new insights, and to grow as individuals. We can analyze what went wrong, identify areas for improvement, and adjust our strategies accordingly.

Failure can also be a powerful motivator. It can ignite a fire within us, a determination to prove ourselves and to overcome the challenges that stand in our way. It can push us to work harder, to think outside the box, and to find creative solutions to problems.

In the words of Thomas Edison, "I have not failed. I've just found 10,000 ways that won't work." Edison's relentless pursuit of the perfect light bulb is a testament to the power of perseverance and the importance of learning from failure.

So, how can we celebrate successes and learn from failures? Here are a few tips:

1. **Acknowledge your wins:** Take the time to celebrate your achievements, no matter how small they may seem. Share your successes with others, and allow yourself to feel proud of what you've accomplished.

2. **Reflect on your experiences:** After each success or failure, take some time to reflect on what you've learned. What worked well? What could you have done differently? What lessons can you apply to future endeavors?

3. **Don't be afraid to fail:** Failure is not the end of the world. It's a learning opportunity, a chance to grow and improve. Embrace failure as a natural part of the journey, and use it as fuel to propel you forward.

4. **Surround yourself with positive people:** Surround yourself with people who believe in you and your dreams. Their support and encouragement will be invaluable during both the highs and lows of your entrepreneurial journey.

5. **Keep learning and growing:** The personal development journey is a constant process of learning and growth. Stay curious, seek out new knowledge, and never stop challenging yourself to improve.

Remember, the journey is not a sprint; it's a marathon. There will be ups and downs, twists and turns, successes and failures. But by celebrating your wins, learning from your losses, and maintaining a positive mindset, you can navigate the challenges, overcome the obstacles, and ultimately achieve your dreams.

As you continue on your entrepreneurial journey, remember to embrace both the successes and the failures. Celebrate your wins, learn from your losses, and never give up on your dreams. The path to success is not always easy, but it is always worth it.

Chapter 4

Learning from Adversity

Let's face it, life isn't always a smooth ride. It throws curveballs, unexpected detours, and sometimes, it feels like a full-blown hurricane. We've all faced adversity in one form or another — setbacks, failures, losses, and challenges that test our resilience and shake us to our core.

But here's the thing: adversity isn't the end. It's not a roadblock, but a stepping stone. It's a catalyst for growth, a teacher that imparts valuable lessons, and a forge that strengthens our character.

In this chapter, we'll delve into the transformative power of adversity. We'll explore how setbacks can become setups for success, how failures can fuel our determination, and how losses can lead us to deeper levels of compassion and understanding.

We'll unpack the strategies I've used to navigate life's storms, from reframing challenges to finding meaning in adversity. We'll discuss the importance of cultivating a resilient mindset, learning from our mistakes, and embracing the growth that comes from facing our fears.

Whether you're currently facing a major challenge or simply want to be better equipped for life's inevitable ups and downs, this chapter is for you. It's a reminder that you're not alone in your struggles, that you have the strength to overcome adversity, and that you can emerge from even the toughest storms stronger and wiser than before.

So, let's dive in and discover how to turn adversity into your greatest advantage.

Reframing adversity as a catalyst for growth.

Life is a series of peaks and valleys, triumphs and setbacks. It's a journey filled with unexpected twists and turns, where adversity often lurks around the corner, ready to test our resilience and challenge our resolve. But what if, instead of viewing adversity as a roadblock, we saw it as a stepping stone? What if we reframed our challenges as opportunities for growth, transformation, and ultimately, triumph?

This is the essence of reframing adversity as a catalyst for growth. It's about shifting our perspective, changing our narrative, and embracing the challenges we face as opportunities to learn, evolve, and become the best versions of ourselves.

Adversity, in its many forms, can be a powerful teacher. It can push us beyond our comfort zones, force us to confront our fears, and reveal our hidden strengths. It can teach us valuable lessons about resilience, perseverance, and the importance of never giving up on our dreams.

In the words of the ancient Stoic philosopher Epictetus, "It's not what happens to you, but how you react to it that matters." This simple yet profound statement encapsulates the essence of reframing adversity. It's not the external circumstances that define us, but our internal response to those circumstances.

When we face adversity, we have a choice. We can either let it defeat us, allowing it to crush our spirits and extinguish our hopes. Or we can choose to rise above it, to use it as fuel for our growth, and to emerge from the experience stronger and more resilient than ever before.

This is not to say that adversity is easy or pleasant. It can be painful, heartbreaking, and even devastating. But it's in these moments of darkness that we have the opportunity to discover our true strength, our resilience, and our capacity for growth.

Think of adversity as a blacksmith's fire. It's intense, it's uncomfortable, but it's also essential for shaping and refining raw materials into something stronger and more valuable. In the same way, adversity can forge us into better versions of ourselves, if we allow it to.

Reframing adversity is not about denying the pain or pretending that everything is okay. It's about acknowledging the challenge, accepting the emotions that come with it, and then choosing to focus on the potential for growth and transformation.

It's about asking ourselves, "What can I learn from this experience? How can I use this challenge to become a better person? What opportunities for growth are hidden within this adversity?"

By asking these questions, we shift our focus from victimhood to empowerment. We take ownership of our circumstances and choose to see them as opportunities rather than obstacles.

Reframing adversity is also about cultivating a growth mindset. This means believing that our abilities and intelligence can be developed through dedication and hard work. It means embracing challenges as opportunities to learn and grow, rather than avoiding them out of fear of failure.

When we adopt a growth mindset, we see setbacks as temporary and failure as a stepping stone to success. We understand that every experience, whether positive or negative, is an opportunity to learn and improve.

The importance of a positive mindset in reframing adversity cannot be overstated. Our thoughts and beliefs shape our reality, and when we choose to focus on the positive, we open ourselves up to new possibilities and opportunities.

A positive mindset doesn't mean ignoring the negative aspects of our lives. It means choosing to focus on the good, to find the silver lining in every cloud, and to believe that we have the power to overcome any challenge.

It means cultivating gratitude, even in the midst of adversity. It means finding joy in the small things, appreciating the present moment, and focusing on what we have rather than what we lack.

A positive mindset is not a magic bullet that will instantly solve all our problems. But it is a powerful tool that can help us navigate through difficult times, find meaning in our struggles, and emerge from adversity stronger and more resilient than ever before.

Personal reflections on overcoming challenges and setbacks.

Life has an uncanny way of testing our resilience, pushing us to our limits, and forcing us to confront our deepest fears. It's in these moments of adversity that we truly discover who we are and what we're made of. My journey has been far from smooth sailing, a turbulent sea of challenges and setbacks that have threatened to capsize my ship time and time again. But through it all, I've learned to navigate the storms, to harness the winds of adversity, and to emerge stronger and more resilient than ever before.

One of the most significant challenges I've faced was the loss of my football dreams. As a young boy, I had poured my heart and soul into the sport, envisioning a future where I would play college ball, maybe even make it to the NFL. But injuries shattered those dreams, leaving me feeling lost and adrift.

The pain of that loss was immense. It was a blow to my identity, my sense of self-worth, and my belief in my own abilities. I felt like I had failed, not just myself but also my family and friends who had supported me along the way.

But as I wallowed in self-pity, I realized that I couldn't let this setback define me. I had to find a new path, a new purpose, a new way to channel my energy and passion. And that's when I discovered my love for art and custom sneakers.

This newfound passion ignited a spark within me, a creative fire that burned brighter than any athletic ambition I had ever known. It was a turning point, a moment of clarity that showed me that even in the face of adversity, there is always hope, always a chance to reinvent yourself and discover new passions.

But perhaps the greatest challenge I've faced was my battle with depression. It was a silent killer, a dark cloud that slowly enveloped me, stealing my joy, my energy, and my will to live. It was a battle fought in the depths of my soul, a struggle against the demons of self-doubt, fear, and despair.

The descent into depression was gradual, insidious. It started with a feeling of unease, a sense of dissatisfaction with my life. Then, slowly but surely, the darkness crept in, casting a shadow over everything I did.

The depression consumed me, leaving me feeling hopeless and helpless. I couldn't see a way out, a light at the end of the tunnel. The pain was unbearable, and the thought of ending my life seemed like the only way to escape it.

The road is long and arduous, but "I'm still standing better than I ever did" haha Elton John reference. I learned to embrace my vulnerability, to ask for help, and to trust in the process of healing. I discovered the power of self-mastery, the importance of forgiveness, and the transformative potential of knowledge. I also found my purpose of leadership, starting my new company The Harry Jones Group, and even writing this book!

Overcoming depression was the greatest challenge I've ever faced, but it was also the most rewarding. It taught me the importance of mental health, the power of resilience, and the opportunities in overcoming. It showed me that even in the darkest of times, there is always hope, always a chance to heal and to thrive.

Strategies for building resilience and strength through adversity.

Adversity is not a roadblock; it's a detour. It's not a dead end; it's a fork in the road. It's not a stop sign; it's a yield sign. It's a test of character, a challenge to our resilience, and an opportunity for growth.

I've faced my fair share of adversity, from financial struggles and racial prejudice to devastating losses and crippling depression. But through it all, I've learned that adversity is not the enemy; it's a teacher, a guide, a catalyst for transformation.

"That which does not kill us makes us stronger." This may sound like a cliché, but it's a truth that I've experienced firsthand. Adversity has the power to break us down, to strip us bare, to expose our vulnerabilities. But it also has the power to build us up, to strengthen our resolve, and to reveal our hidden strengths.

So, how do we harness the power of adversity and use it to build resilience and strength? Here are a few strategies that have worked for me:

1. **Reframe Your Perspective:** Adversity is not something that happens to us; it's something we interpret. Our perception of adversity shapes our response to it. Instead of viewing adversity as a punishment or a setback, try to see it as a

challenge, an opportunity for growth, or a test of your resilience.

2. **Embrace Your Emotions:** It's okay to feel sad, angry, or frustrated when faced with adversity. Don't try to suppress your emotions; allow yourself to feel them fully. But don't let them consume you. Acknowledge your emotions, process them, and then let them go.

3. **Seek Support:** You don't have to go through adversity alone. Reach out to your friends, family, therapist, mentor or spiritual advisor. Talk about what you're going through, share your feelings, and ask for help. A strong support system can make all the difference in your ability to cope with adversity.

4. **Focus on What You Can Control:** When faced with adversity, it's easy to feel overwhelmed and powerless. But there are always things you can control, even in the most difficult situations. Focus on your actions, your attitude, and your choices. Take small steps each day to move forward, even if it's just getting out of bed or taking a shower.

5. **Find Meaning in Your Suffering:** Meaning that "those who have a 'why' to live, can bear with almost any 'how'." Finding meaning in your suffering can give you the strength to endure even the most difficult challenges.

6. **Practice Gratitude:** Even in the midst of adversity, there is always something to be grateful for. Take time each day to reflect on the good things in your life, no matter how small

they may seem. Gratitude can shift your focus from what you lack to what you have, and it can help you to cultivate a more positive outlook.

7. **Cultivate a Growth Mindset:** A growth mindset is the belief that your abilities and intelligence can be developed through dedication and hard work. This mindset is essential for overcoming adversity because it allows you to see challenges as opportunities for growth rather than threats to your self-esteem.

8. **Take Care of Yourself:** Adversity can take a toll on your physical and mental health. Make sure you're getting enough sleep, eating nutritious foods, and exercising regularly. Take time for relaxation and self-care.

9. **Don't Give Up:** Resilience is not about never falling down; it's about getting back up again and again. When faced with adversity, it's easy to feel discouraged and want to give up. But remember, every setback is an opportunity to learn and grow. Keep moving forward, one step at a time, and never lose sight of your goals.

Remember, adversity is not the end of the road; it's a bend in the road. It's an opportunity to learn, to grow, and to become a stronger, more resilient version of yourself. Embrace the challenges, learn from your mistakes, and never give up on your dreams.

As the saying goes, "Smooth seas do not make skillful sailors." It's the storms we weather that shape us into the capable and resilient individuals we are meant to be. So, embrace the adversity, for it is in the face of challenges that we truly discover our strength.

The role of mindset and perspective in dealing with difficult situations.

Life is a series of peaks and valleys, a constant ebb and flow of wins and losses. It's how we navigate these difficult situations that truly defines us. Our mindset, the lens through which we view the world, plays a crucial role in our ability to cope with adversity, overcome obstacles, and ultimately thrive.

In the depths of my depression, my mindset was my worst enemy. I saw the world through a lens of negativity, focusing on my failures, my shortcomings, and the injustices I had faced. I was trapped in a cycle of self-doubt and despair, unable to see a way out.

But as I began my journey of personal development and spiritual growth, I realized that my mindset was not fixed, it was malleable. I had the power to change my perspective, to reframe my experiences, and to choose a more empowering narrative.

One of the most transformative shifts in my mindset was embracing the concept of abundance versus scarcity. Instead of focusing on what I lacked, I started to focus on what I had. Instead of seeing limitations, I started to see possibilities. This shift in perspective opened up a whole new world of opportunities and possibilities.

I also learned the importance of controlling the controllables. In the face of adversity, it's easy to feel overwhelmed and powerless. But by focusing on the things we can control – our thoughts, our actions, our attitudes – we can regain a sense of dominion and empowerment.

Another key aspect of mastering my mind was learning to challenge my negative self-talk. I realized that the voice in my head was not always my friend. It often whispered lies, doubts, and fears, undermining my confidence and sabotaging my efforts.

By becoming aware of my negative self-talk and consciously choosing to replace it with positive affirmations, I was able to reprogram my subconscious mind and cultivate a more optimistic outlook.

The power of perspective cannot be overstated. Our perspective shapes our reality, influencing how we interpret events, how we react to challenges, and how we perceive ourselves and the world around us.

When we adopt a positive perspective, we see opportunities where others see obstacles. We find strength in adversity, resilience in setbacks, and lessons in failures. We approach life with a sense of optimism, hope, and possibility.

On the other hand, a negative perspective can be incredibly destructive. It can blind us to opportunities, magnify our challenges, and keep us trapped in a cycle of self-doubt and despair. It can lead to feelings of helplessness, hopelessness, and ultimately, defeat.

The good news is that we have the power to choose our perspective. We can choose to focus on the positive, to see the good in every situation, and to believe in our ability to overcome any obstacle.

This is not to say that we should ignore or deny the challenges we face. It's important to acknowledge our pain, our struggles, and our setbacks. But we don't have to let them define us. We can choose to see them as opportunities for growth, as stepping stones on our journey towards a better future.

The role of mindset and perspective in dealing with difficult situations is undeniable. By cultivating a positive mindset, we can transform our challenges into opportunities, our setbacks into stepping stones, and our failures into lessons. We can find strength in adversity, resilience in setbacks, and hope in the face of despair.

We always have a choice. We can choose to let our circumstances define us, or we can choose to rise above them. We can choose to see the world through a lens of negativity and despair, or we can choose to see it through a lens of hope and possibility.

The choice is ours. And the power of our choice is limitless.

Finding meaning and purpose in adversity.

Adversity, a formidable foe that tests our resilience, challenges our beliefs, and pushes us to the brink of despair. It's the storm that threatens to uproot us, the darkness that obscures our path, the weight that threatens to crush our spirits. But what if, instead of viewing adversity as a curse, we saw it as a catalyst for growth, a crucible for transformation, a stepping stone to a more meaningful and purposeful life?

In the depths of my own struggles, I discovered that adversity, while painful and challenging, can also be a powerful teacher. It can reveal our hidden strengths, expose our vulnerabilities, and force us to confront our deepest fears. It can shatter our illusions, challenge our assumptions, and push us to re-evaluate our priorities.

The loss of my football dreams, the financial hardships, failed businesses, the descent into depression—each of these adversities tested me in ways I never could have imagined. They pushed me to my limits, forcing me to confront my deepest fears and insecurities.

But in the midst of the pain and suffering, I also discovered a resilience within myself that I never knew existed. I learned that I was stronger than I thought, more capable than I had ever imagined. I found that even in the darkest of times, there was a flicker of hope, a spark of determination that refused to be extinguished.

Through adversity, I discovered the importance of gratitude. In the midst of my struggles, I learned to appreciate the simple things in life—the warmth of the sun on my face, the sound of laughter, the love and support of my family and

friends. I realized that even in the darkest of times, there was always something to be grateful for.

Adversity also taught me the importance of perspective. When we're in the thick of it, it's easy to get caught up in the negativity, to focus on what's going wrong. But by shifting our perspective, by looking for the lessons and opportunities hidden within the challenges, we can transform adversity into a catalyst for growth.

I once heard "Everything can be taken from a man but one thing: the last of human freedoms—to choose one's attitude in any given set of circumstances, to choose one's own way."

These words resonated with me deeply. I realized that even in the face of unimaginable suffering, we still have the power to choose our response. We can choose to succumb to despair or to find meaning and purpose in our pain.

For me, finding meaning in adversity meant using my experiences to help others. It meant sharing my story, my struggles, and my triumphs, in the hope that it would inspire others to overcome their own challenges.

It meant creating the Harry Jones Group, a platform dedicated to empowering people to develop resilience, overcome adversity, and achieve their full potential. It meant using my pain as a catalyst for positive change in the world.

Finding purpose in adversity is not about denying the pain or pretending that everything is okay. It's about acknowledging the suffering, learning from it, and using it as fuel for growth. It's about finding the silver lining in the storm clouds, the lessons hidden within the challenges.

It's about realizing that adversity is not a roadblock, but a detour, a different path that can lead us to unexpected destinations. It's about embracing the journey, with all its twists and turns, and trusting that it will ultimately lead us to a place of greater strength, wisdom, and purpose.

The importance of self-compassion and forgiveness.

In the depths of my despair, as I grappled with the weight of my past mistakes and the pain I had caused myself and others, I discovered a powerful tool for healing and growth: self-compassion. It was a concept that I had never fully grasped before, a radical act of kindness towards oneself that I had long neglected.

For years, I had been my own harshest critic, berating myself for my failures, my shortcomings, and my perceived inadequacies. I had internalized the negative messages I had received from others, believing that I was not good enough, not smart enough, not worthy of love and happiness.

This self-flagellation had become a toxic habit, a constant loop of negative self-talk that eroded my self-esteem and fueled my depression. I was trapped in a cycle of self-blame and shame, unable to see a way out.

But as I began to explore the concept of self-compassion, I realized that I had been treating myself with a cruelty that I would never inflict on others. I had been holding myself to an impossible standard of perfection, expecting myself to be flawless in every way.

Self-compassion involves treating ourselves with kindness and understanding, rather than judgment and criticism. It means recognizing that we are all imperfect, that we all make mistakes, and that we all deserve love and compassion, especially from ourselves.

Embracing self-compassion was not easy. It required me to challenge my deeply ingrained beliefs about myself, to let go of shortcomings, and to accept my flaws and work on what I could.

I started by practicing mindfulness, paying attention to my thoughts and feelings without judgment. I learned to recognize the negative self-talk that had become so ingrained in my mind, and to replace it with positive affirmations and words of encouragement.

I also started practicing self-care, prioritizing my physical and emotional well-being. I made time for activities that brought me joy, such as spending time in nature, working out, and building business. I learned to nourish my body with healthy food and exercise, and to prioritize rest and relaxation.

As I cultivated self-compassion, I began to experience a profound shift in my relationship with myself. I became less critical, more forgiving, and more accepting of my imperfections. I started to see myself as a whole person, with strengths and weaknesses, rather than a collection of flaws and failures.

This shift in perspective had a ripple effect on all areas of my life. I became more confident, more resilient, and more compassionate towards others. I was able to forgive myself for my past mistakes, to let go of the shame and guilt that had been holding me back, and to move forward with a renewed sense of purpose.

Along with self-compassion, I also learned the importance of forgiveness. For years, I had harbored resentment towards those who had hurt me, blaming them for my struggles and misfortunes. But I realized that holding onto anger and resentment was only hurting me. It was like drinking poison and expecting the other person to die.

Forgiveness, I discovered, is not about condoning or excusing the actions of others. It's about freeing ourselves from the burden of anger and resentment, so that we can move forward with peace and grace.

I started by forgiving myself for my past mistakes. I acknowledged the pain I had caused myself and others, and I made a conscious decision to let go of the guilt and shame. I realized that I had done the best I could with the knowledge and resources I had at the time, and that I deserved forgiveness, just as I had forgiven others.

I then turned my attention to forgiving those who had hurt me. It wasn't easy, but I realized that holding onto anger and resentment was only poisoning my own heart. I wrote letters to those who had wronged me, expressing my pain and anger, but also offering forgiveness. I didn't expect them to apologize or make amends; I simply wanted to release myself from the burden of carrying their offenses.

The act of forgiveness was incredibly liberating. It felt like a weight had been lifted from my shoulders, a dark cloud lifted from my heart. I was no longer defined by the pain of the past; I was free to move forward with love and compassion.

The journey of self-compassion and forgiveness is ongoing, a lifelong practice of self-reflection, growth, and healing. But the rewards are immeasurable. By learning to love and forgive ourselves, we open ourselves up to a world of possibilities. We become more resilient, more compassionate, and more capable of creating a life that is truly our own.

Turning pain into power and using experiences to help others.

The depths of despair I had plunged into were not in vain. They were, in hindsight, the fertile ground from which my most profound transformation would sprout. The pain, the loss, the feelings of utter hopelessness—they were not the end, but rather the raw materials for a new beginning.

During my depression, I had stumbled upon a universal truth: pain is inevitable, but suffering is optional. We cannot control the events that happen to us, but we can control how we respond to them. We can choose to let pain break us, or we can choose to let it make us.

I made a conscious decision to turn my pain into power. I refused to let my struggles define me. Instead, I used them as fuel for growth, as a catalyst for change. I embraced my experiences, both the good and the bad, as valuable lessons that had shaped me into the person I was becoming.

I realized that my story, my journey through darkness and despair, had the power to inspire and uplift others. I had a unique perspective to offer, a message of hope and resilience that could resonate with those who were struggling.

And so, I began to share my story. I spoke openly and honestly about my battles with depression, anxiety, and failure. I shared the raw, unfiltered truth of my experiences, the pain, the shame, the fear.

At first, it was terrifying. I felt vulnerable and exposed, like I was laying my soul bare for the world to see. But as I shared my story, I realized that I was not alone. There were countless others who had faced similar challenges, who had felt the same pain, who had struggled with the same demons.

My story resonated with them, and they found solace and strength in knowing that they were not alone. They saw themselves in my struggles, and they were inspired by my resilience.

As I continued to share my story, I discovered that my pain had a purpose. It was not meant to break me; it was meant to empower me to help others. My experiences had given me a unique ability to connect with people on a deep level, to empathize with their struggles, and to offer them hope and guidance.

I realized that I had a gift, a calling to use my experiences to make a positive impact on the world. I had a responsibility to share my story, to offer hope to those who were struggling, and to empower them to overcome their own challenges.

And so, I embraced my pain, my struggles, my experiences, and turned them into a source of power. I used them to fuel my passion for helping others, to inspire them to believe in themselves, and to create a life of purpose and meaning.

I founded the Harry Jones Group, an organization dedicated to empowering people to overcome adversity and achieve their full potential. Through workshops, seminars, and online resources, we provide young people with the tools and support they need to navigate the challenges of life.

We teach them about the importance of mindset, the power of resilience, and the transformative skills necessary to succeed. We share our own stories of overcoming adversity, and we provide a safe and supportive space for them to share their own struggles.

Our mission is to empower people to believe in themselves, to embrace their challenges, and to create a life that is filled with joy, purpose, and meaning. We believe that every person has the potential to achieve greatness, and we are committed to helping them unlock that potential.

Turning pain into power is not an easy process. It requires courage, vulnerability, and a willingness to confront our deepest fears and insecurities.

But it is a process that is ultimately rewarding, one that can lead to profound personal growth and transformation.

By embracing our pain, we can find meaning in our suffering, connect with others on a deeper level, and use our experiences to make a positive impact on the world. We can turn our wounds into wisdom, our scars into badges of honor, and our pain into power.

Celebrating resilience and using adversity as a stepping stone to success.

The trials and tribulations I faced, the setbacks and heartbreaks, were not in vain. They were the crucible in which my resilience was forged, the catalyst for my personal growth, and the stepping stones that led me to success.

Each adversity I encountered, each obstacle I overcame, strengthened my resolve and deepened my understanding of myself and the world around me. The financial struggles of my childhood taught me the value of hard work, resourcefulness, and the importance of financial literacy. The racial prejudice I experienced fueled my determination to break down barriers and create a more equitable society. The loss of loved ones taught me the preciousness of life, the importance of cherishing relationships, and the power of turning pain into purpose.

My journey has been far from easy, but it has been incredibly rewarding. I've learned that adversity is not a roadblock, but a detour, a different path that can lead to unexpected destinations. It's a test of our character, our resilience, and our ability to adapt and overcome.

Resilience, the ability to bounce back from setbacks and challenges, is not a trait we are born with; it's a skill we develop through experience. It's the ability to pick ourselves up when we fall, to dust ourselves off, and to keep moving forward, even when the road ahead seems uncertain.

Resilience is not about ignoring the pain or pretending that everything is okay. It's about acknowledging the pain, processing it, and using it as fuel for growth. It's about finding the strength to carry on, even when we feel like we can't take another step.

Adversity can be a powerful teacher, if we are willing to learn from it. It can teach us about our strengths and weaknesses, our values and priorities, our hopes and dreams. It can show us what we're truly capable of, and it can push us to become the best version of ourselves.

But adversity is not just about overcoming challenges; it's also about using those challenges as stepping stones to success. It's about taking the lessons we've learned, the strength we've gained, and the wisdom we've acquired, and using them to create a better future for ourselves and for others.

I've learned that adversity can be a catalyst for innovation, a spark that ignites our creativity and resourcefulness. It can force us to think outside the box, to find new solutions to old problems, and to create something truly unique and valuable.

My own experiences with adversity have led me to create The Harry Jones Group, a company dedicated to empowering young people to overcome challenges and achieve their full potential. Through our programs and services, we provide young people with the tools and resources they need to navigate the complexities of life, to develop resilience, and to create a brighter future for themselves and their communities. Ya know the things we should learn young.

Celebrating resilience and using adversity as a stepping stone to success is not just about overcoming challenges; it's about embracing them as opportunities for growth and transformation. It's about recognizing that our struggles do not define us, but rather, they shape us into the resilient, compassionate, and empowered individuals we are meant to be.

So, let us celebrate our resilience, let us embrace our challenges, and let us use adversity as a stepping stone to success. Let us remember that we are not defined by our struggles, but by our ability to overcome them. Let us rise above the ashes, stronger and more determined than ever before, and create a life that is truly our own.

CHAPTER 5

FINDING TRUE PURPOSE

Ever had that nagging feeling that there's something more to life than the daily grind? A sense that you're meant for something bigger, something that ignites your soul and leaves a lasting impact? If so, you're not alone.

The journey to discovering our true purpose is a universal human quest. It's a yearning to understand why we're here, what our unique gifts and talents are, and how we can use them to make a difference in the world. It's about aligning our passions with our actions, our dreams with our reality, and our individual selves with the greater whole.

But finding our true purpose isn't always a straightforward path. It's often a winding road filled with detours, roadblocks, and unexpected turns. It can be a process of trial and error, of exploring different avenues and experimenting with various possibilities. It requires us to look inward, to question our assumptions, and to challenge our limiting beliefs.

In this chapter, we'll embark on a journey of self-discovery, exploring the depths of our being to uncover our true calling. We'll delve into the importance of aligning our passions and talents with our purpose, of overcoming societal expectations and pressures, and of trusting our intuition and inner guidance. We'll discuss the significance of serving others and making a positive impact, of living a purpose-driven life and finding fulfillment in the process.

Through personal anecdotes, practical exercises, and insightful reflections, we'll navigate the complexities of finding our true purpose and living a life that is both meaningful and rewarding. We'll uncover the hidden potential that lies within each of us, and we'll discover the joy and satisfaction that comes from living a life that is aligned with our deepest values and aspirations.

So, are you ready to embark on this exciting journey of self-discovery? Are you ready to unlock the secrets of your true purpose and create a life that is filled with passion, meaning, and impact? If so, let's dive in and explore the limitless possibilities that await us.

The journey of self-discovery and finding one's true calling.

The path to discovering one's true purpose is rarely a straight line. It's a winding road filled with twists, turns, and unexpected detours. It's a journey of self-exploration, of peeling back the layers of societal expectations and conditioning to uncover the authentic self that lies beneath.

For me, this journey began in the aftermath of my darkest hour. As I emerged from the depths of depression, I realized that I had been living a life that wasn't truly my own. I had been chasing external validation, seeking fulfillment, a vision that wasn't mine and fleeting pleasures. But it was all a facade, a mask I wore to hide the pain and emptiness that ate at my soul.

In the silence of my darkness, I began to ask myself the hard questions: Who am I? What do I truly want out of life? What is my purpose? These questions, once buried beneath layers of fear and self-doubt, now demanded to be answered.

I embarked on a journey of self-discovery, a quest to uncover my true calling. I started by exploring my passions and interests. I began to heal myself physically through training and nutrition. I also dove into personal development, reading books, listening to podcasts, and seminars on topics like mindset, spirituality, and purpose. My goal was to heal myself from my pain and become the person I admire most in all areas of my life.

Through this process of self-exploration, I began to see myself in a new light. I discovered hidden talents and untapped potential. I realized that I had a unique perspective to offer the world, a story to share, a message to convey.

But finding my true calling wasn't just about discovering my passions and talents; it was also about aligning them with my values and beliefs. It was about finding my gifts, refining my gifts and using them to serve others, to make a positive impact on the world.

This realization led me to create The Harry Jones Group, an educational company dedicated to empowering young people to overcome adversity and achieve their full potential. Finding my true calling was not a eureka moment, but rather a gradual unfolding, a process of self-discovery and alignment. It was about listening to my intuition, following my heart, working hard, and following God on the journey.

It was also about letting go of expectations and pressures. I had to shed the limiting beliefs that had been ingrained in me from a young age, the idea that I had to follow a certain path to be successful. I had to embrace my individuality, my unique gifts, and my own definition of success.

The journey of self-discovery is not always easy. It can be messy, confusing, and at times, downright terrifying. But it is also incredibly rewarding. It is a journey that leads us to our authentic selves, to our true purpose, and to a life of fulfillment and meaning.

If you are on a journey to find your true calling, I encourage you to embrace the process. Explore your passions, listen to your intuition, and don't be afraid to step outside of your comfort zone. Remember, your purpose is not something you find; it's something you create. It's about aligning your passions, talents, and values with a cause that is greater than yourself.

As the author and motivational speaker, Steve Maraboli, once said, "The purpose of life is not to be happy. It is to be useful, to be honorable, to be compassionate, to have it make some difference that you have lived and lived well."

Your true calling is waiting for you. It's time to discover it, embrace it, and share it with the world.

The importance of aligning passions and talents with purpose.

In the pursuit of our true purpose, it's essential to recognize the profound connection between our passions, talents, and the deeper meaning we seek in life. When these elements align, we unlock a wellspring of fulfillment, joy, and impact.

Passions: The Fuel of Our Souls

Passions are the fiery embers that ignite our souls, the driving forces that propel us forward. They are the activities, interests, or causes that make our hearts race, our minds buzz, and our spirits soar. Passions are not merely hobbies or fleeting interests; they are deeply ingrained desires that reflect our authentic selves.

When we engage in activities we are passionate about, we tap into a source of energy and enthusiasm that is both exhilarating and fulfilling. We lose track of time, immerse ourselves fully in the present moment, and experience a sense of flow that is both effortless and invigorating.

Passions are not just about pleasure; they are also about purpose. They connect us to something larger than ourselves, something that gives our lives meaning and significance. When we pursue our passions, we tap into our innate gifts and talents, using them to make a positive impact on the world.

Talents: Our Unique Gifts

Talents are our natural abilities, the skills and strengths that come easily to us. They are the things we excel at, the activities that make us feel alive and engaged. Talents are not just about what we are good at; they are also about what we enjoy doing.

When we use our talents, we tap into a source of creativity and innovation. We are able to express ourselves authentically, to share our unique gifts with the world, and to make a meaningful contribution to society.

Talents are not just about personal fulfillment; they are also about service. When we use our talents to help others, we experience a deep sense of satisfaction and purpose. We realize that our gifts are not just for our own benefit, but also for the betterment of humanity.

Purpose: The Intersection of Passion and Talent

Purpose is the sweet spot where our passions and talents intersect. It's the reason we get out of bed in the morning, the driving force behind our actions, the guiding light that illuminates our path.

When we align our passions and talents with our purpose, we create a life that is both fulfilling and impactful. We are able to use our unique gifts to make a difference in the world, to leave a lasting legacy, and to experience a deep sense of satisfaction and joy.

Finding our purpose is not always easy. It requires self-reflection, exploration, and a willingness to step outside of our comfort zones. But the rewards are immeasurable. When we live a purpose-driven life, we tap into a source of energy and motivation that is both sustainable and fulfilling.

The Importance of Alignment

Aligning our passions and talents with our purpose is not just about personal fulfillment; it's also about maximizing our impact on the world. When we are passionate about what we do, we are more likely to be engaged, motivated, and persistent in our efforts. When we use our talents, we are more likely to be creative, innovative, and effective in our work.

When our passions, talents, and purpose are aligned, we become a force to be reckoned with. We are able to achieve great things, to make a real difference in the world, and to leave a lasting legacy.

Practical Steps to Align Your Passions and Talents with Purpose

1. **Identify Your Passions:** What are the activities, interests, or causes that light you up? What do you love to do, even if you don't get paid for it?

2. **Discover Your Talents:** What are your natural abilities? What skills and strengths come easily to you? What do you excel at?

3. **Explore Your Purpose:** What is your why? What impact do you want to make on the world? What legacy do you want to leave behind?

4. **Find the Intersection:** Look for ways to combine your passions and talents in a way that serves your purpose. What unique contribution can you make to the world?

5. **Take Action:** Don't just dream about it; do it! Start taking small steps towards aligning your passions and talents with your purpose.

Remember, finding your purpose is a journey, not a destination. It's an ongoing process of self-discovery, growth, and evolution. But by aligning your passions and talents with your purpose, you can create a life that is both fulfilling and impactful. You can unlock your full potential and make a real difference in the world.

Overcoming societal expectations and pressures.

From a young age, I felt the weight of societal expectations pressing down on me. Growing up in a low-income Black family in a predominantly white town, the path to success seemed narrow and predefined. The messages I received from society were clear: get good grades, go to college, get a stable job, and follow the well-trodden path laid out before me, go to the NFL, rap, or sell drugs.

But deep down, I knew there was more to life than conforming to these expectations. I felt a yearning for something different, something that would ignite my soul and set me on a path of true fulfillment.

The pressure to conform was immense. My family, teachers, and peers all had their own ideas of what I should do with my life. They encouraged me to pursue traditional careers, to prioritize financial stability over passion and purpose.

I remember the countless conversations about college majors, career paths, and the importance of "being realistic." I felt like I was being pushed into a mold that didn't fit, a life that didn't resonate with my true desires.

The weight of these expectations was suffocating. I felt like I was betraying myself, sacrificing my dreams for the sake of societal approval. I was caught in a tug-of-war between my own aspirations and the expectations of others.

But amidst the pressure, a small voice within me whispered, "Don't settle." It was a voice that urged me to break free from the mold, to forge my own path, to create a life that was authentically mine.

The journey of overcoming societal expectations was not an easy one. It required me to question everything I had been taught, to challenge the status quo, and to trust my own intuition. It was a journey of self-discovery, of shedding the layers of conditioning that had been imposed upon me, and of embracing my unique individuality.

I started by exploring my passions and interests. I delved into art, fashion, and entrepreneurship, experimenting with different mediums and styles. I read books, and watched youtube videos of mentors who had forged their own paths.

Through this process of exploration, I discovered a passion for custom sneakers and artwork. It was a passion that ignited my soul, a creative outlet that allowed me to express myself in a way that felt authentic and true.

But pursuing my passion was not without its challenges. I faced skepticism and discouragement from those who believed I was wasting my time and talent. They urged me to focus on "practical" pursuits, to get a "real" job, to conform to their expectations of what a successful life looked like.

But I refused to let their doubts deter me. I knew that my passion was more than just a hobby; it was a calling, a purpose that I was meant to fulfill. I had to trust my intuition, to believe in myself, and to have the courage to pursue my dreams, even in the face of opposition.

Overcoming societal expectations required me to develop a strong sense of self-worth and self-belief. I had to learn to value my own opinions, my own desires, and my own unique path. I had to silence the voices of doubt and criticism, both internal and external, and to trust my own inner guidance.

It was a process of unlearning and relearning, of shedding the layers of conditioning that had been imposed upon me and of embracing my authentic self. It was a journey of self-discovery, of finding my own voice, and of creating a life that was true to my values and aspirations.

The journey of overcoming societal expectations is an ongoing one. There will always be pressures to conform, to follow the crowd, to fit into a mold that doesn't quite fit. But by staying true to ourselves, by trusting our intuition, and by having the courage to pursue our passions, we can break free from the limitations imposed upon us and create a life that is truly our own.

The role of intuition and inner guidance in discovering purpose.

In the grand symphony of life, our intuition is the subtle melody that often gets drowned out by the blaring trumpets of external noise and societal expectations. It's that quiet whisper in the back of our minds, that gut feeling that nudges us in a certain direction, that inexplicable knowing that guides us towards our true path.

Intuition, often referred to as our "authentic voice of God," is a powerful tool that can help us navigate the complexities of life and discover our true purpose. It's that innate wisdom that resides within each of us, a compass that points us towards our North Star.

But in a world that constantly bombards us with information, opinions, and distractions, it can be difficult to hear the subtle whispers of our intuition. We're often so caught up in the external noise that we lose touch with our inner voice, the one that knows us better than anyone else.

Rediscovering and trusting our intuition is a journey of self-discovery, a process of peeling back the layers of conditioning and societal expectations to uncover the authentic self that lies beneath. It's about learning to listen to our bodies, our hearts, and our souls, and to trust the wisdom that resides within.

For me, the journey of discovering my true purpose was deeply intertwined with the rediscovery of my intuition. After years of being unhealthy and suppressing my inner voice, of trying to fit into a mold that wasn't meant for me, I finally reached a breaking point.

It was during my darkest hour, when I was battling depression and contemplating suicide, that I realized the importance of listening to my intuition. It was a faint whisper at first, a gentle nudge in a different direction. But as I started to pay attention, to quiet the noise of the world and tune into wisdom, the whisper grew louder, more insistent.

It was my intuition that guided me towards personal development that led me to seek help from mentors. It was my intuition that nudged me to reconnect with my faith, to explore my creativity, and to start leading with purpose.

As I learned to trust my intuition, I began to see the world through a new lens. I realized that my purpose wasn't something I had to find; it was something I had to uncover, to unearth from within. It was a journey of self-discovery, a process of peeling back the layers to reveal the authentic self that had been there all along.

Intuition is not a magical power or a mystical gift; it's a natural human ability that we all possess. It's the culmination of our experiences, our knowledge, and our subconscious wisdom. It's the voice of our soul, guiding us towards our highest good.

But like any muscle, intuition needs to be exercised and strengthened. It requires us to quiet our minds, to listen to our bodies, and to trust our gut feelings. It requires us to be open to new possibilities, to embrace the unknown, and to follow the path that feels right, even if it goes against conventional wisdom.

The role of intuition in discovering purpose is not about following a predetermined path or fulfilling someone else's expectations. It's about aligning your actions with your conscience.

It's about recognizing that your purpose is not something you find outside of yourself; it's something that you uncover from within.

Once you do, It's about refining it, then deploying it into the world to leave a positive impact.

As you embark on your own journey of discovering your true purpose, I encourage you to listen to your intuition. Trust that inner voice that whispers to you, that nudges you in a certain direction. Be open to new possibilities, embrace the unknown, and follow the path that feels right for you.

Remember, your intuition is your most powerful ally on this journey. It's the compass that will guide you towards your North Star, the light that will illuminate your path, and the wisdom that will lead you to your true purpose.

Living a purpose-driven life and finding fulfillment.

Discovering your true purpose is just the beginning. The real magic happens when you start living a purpose-driven life, a life that is aligned with your values, passions, and unique gifts. It's about waking up each day with a sense of excitement and fulfillment, knowing that you're making a difference in your world.

Living a purpose-driven life is not about chasing external validation or material possessions. It's about finding meaning and fulfillment in the work you do, the relationships you cultivate, and the impact you have on others. It's about living a life that is authentic, intentional, and aligned with your deepest values.

So, how do you live a purpose-driven life? It starts with clarifying your values. What is important to you? What do you stand for?

What kind of impact do you want to have on the world? Once you have a clear understanding of your values, you can start to make choices that are aligned with them.

Next, identify your passions. What are you naturally drawn to? What activities make you lose track of time? What do you love learning about? Your passions are clues to your purpose, signposts pointing you in the right direction.

Finally, consider your unique gifts and talents. What are you good at? What comes naturally to you? What do others admire about you? Your gifts are not random; they are tools that you can use to serve others and make a positive impact on the world.

Once you have a clear understanding of your values, passions, and gifts, you can start to explore different ways to express them in your life. This could involve volunteering your time to a cause you care about, starting a business that aligns with your values, or simply incorporating your passions into your daily routine.

Living a purpose-driven life is not always easy. It requires courage, commitment, and a willingness to step outside of your comfort zone. But the rewards are immeasurable. When you live a life that is aligned with your purpose, you experience a deep sense of fulfillment, joy, and satisfaction.

You wake up each day with a sense of excitement and anticipation, eager to tackle the challenges and opportunities that lie ahead. You feel a sense of connection to something bigger than yourself, a sense of meaning and purpose that transcends the mundane.

Living a purpose-driven life is also about making a positive impact on the world. When you use your gifts and talents to serve others, you create a ripple effect of positivity that extends far beyond yourself. You inspire others to live their own purpose-driven lives, and you contribute to the greater good of humanity.

Finding fulfillment in life is not about achieving a certain level of success or accumulating material possessions. It's about living a life that is aligned with your values, passions, and purpose. It's about making a difference in the world and leaving a lasting legacy.

As you embark on your journey to live a purpose-driven life, remember that it's not about perfection. It's about progress, about taking small steps each day towards your goals. It's about embracing the challenges, learning from your mistakes, and never giving up on your dreams.

Surround yourself with people who support and encourage you. Seek out mentors who can guide you on your path.

Living a purpose-driven life is a journey, not a destination. It's a lifelong process of self-discovery, growth, and contribution. But it's a journey that is worth taking, for it is the path to true fulfillment and happiness.

The importance of continuous growth and evolution.

The journey to discovering and fulfilling our true purpose is not a destination but an ongoing process of growth and evolution. It's a dynamic dance between our inner selves and the ever-changing world around us. It's about constantly pushing our boundaries, expanding our horizons, and embracing new experiences that challenge us to become better versions of ourselves.

Think of it like a tree reaching for the sky. It starts as a tiny seed, buried in the earth, with the potential for greatness locked within. With time, nourishment, and the right conditions, it sprouts, grows, and eventually reaches its full potential, its branches reaching towards the heavens.

But even then, the tree doesn't stop growing. It continues to adapt to its environment, its roots digging deeper, its branches reaching wider. It sheds its leaves in the fall, only to bloom again in the spring, a symbol of renewal and resilience.

Similarly, our personal growth is a continuous process. We are never truly finished, never fully formed. There is always more to learn, more to experience, more to become.

Embracing continuous growth means stepping outside of our comfort zones, challenging our assumptions, and being open to new ideas and perspectives. It means recognizing that we are not perfect, that we will make mistakes, but that those mistakes are valuable learning opportunities.

It means cultivating a growth mindset, a belief that our abilities and intelligence can be developed through dedication and hard work. It means embracing challenges as opportunities for growth, rather than threats to our ego.

Continuous growth also means evolving our understanding of our purpose. As we learn and grow, our passions and interests may shift, and our definition of success may change. It's important to be flexible and adaptable, to allow our purpose to evolve along with us.

This doesn't mean abandoning our core values or compromising our integrity. It simply means recognizing that our journey is not linear, that there will be twists and turns along the way. It means embracing the uncertainty and trusting that we are being guided towards our highest good.

The importance of continuous growth and evolution cannot be overstated. It is essential for our personal fulfillment, our professional success, and our overall well-being.

When we stop growing, we stagnate. We become complacent, stuck in our routines, and resistant to change. We lose our sense of curiosity, our passion for learning, and our zest for life.

But when we embrace growth, we open ourselves up to a world of possibilities. We discover new talents, new interests, and new ways of being. We become more resilient, more adaptable, and more capable of handling life's challenges.

Continuous growth also allows us to make a greater impact on the world. As we expand our knowledge and skills, we become better equipped to serve others, to contribute to our communities, and to make a positive difference in the world.

Think of the people who have inspired you the most. Chances are, they are individuals who have dedicated themselves to lifelong learning and growth. They are constantly seeking new knowledge, new experiences, and new ways to make a difference.

They are not afraid to challenge the status quo, to question conventional wisdom, and to forge their own path. They are driven by a deep sense of purpose, a desire to leave their mark on the world.

By embracing continuous growth and evolution, we can follow in their footsteps. We can become the best versions of ourselves, live a life of purpose and meaning, and make a lasting impact on the world.

Remember, the journey of self-discovery is not a sprint; it's a marathon. It's a lifelong process of learning, growing, and evolving. Embrace the journey, embrace the challenges, and embrace the endless possibilities that await you.

The rewards of finding and living our true purpose are immeasurable. It brings a sense of fulfillment, joy, and meaning to our lives. It allows us to connect with others on a deeper level, to make a positive impact on the world, and to leave a lasting legacy.

So, how can we find our true purpose? There is no one-size-fits-all answer, but there are some key steps we can take:

1. **Become the person you admire most and give it to the world:** What are qualities you admire most? What are you struggling most with? Whatever you can overcome you can help others do the same.

2. **Reflect on your passions and talents:** What are you naturally drawn to? What activities make you lose track of time? What are you good at?

3. **Explore your values and beliefs:** What is important to you? What do you stand for? What kind of impact do you want to make on the world?

4. **Listen to your intuition:** What is your gut telling you? What feels right in your heart?

5. **Take action:** Don't be afraid to experiment, to try new things, and to step outside of your comfort zone.

6. **Seek guidance:** Talk to mentors, coaches, or therapists who can help you clarify your goals and develop a plan of action.

Remember, finding your true purpose is not a destination; it's a journey. It's an ongoing process of self-discovery, growth, and evolution. Embrace the journey, trust the process, and allow your purpose to unfold organically.

CHAPTER 6

BE DO HAVE

We're about to dive into a concept that has the power to revolutionize your life: the Be Do Have principle. This isn't some new-age mumbo jumbo; it's a timeless truth that has been guiding humanity for centuries. It's a simple yet profound formula that can unlock your full potential and lead you to a life of abundance and fulfillment.

In essence, the Be Do Have principle states that your being determines your doing, which in turn determines your having. In other words, who you are at your core shapes your actions, and your actions ultimately shape your results.

Sounds pretty straightforward, right? But here's the kicker: most of us have it backward. We focus on the "having" – the material possessions, the external validation, the pleasures – thinking that once we have those things, we'll finally be happy and fulfilled.

But the truth is, happiness and fulfillment come from within. They arise from aligning our being with our doing, from living a life of integrity and purpose.

This chapter is divided into three subchapters to help you master the Be Do Have principle:

1. **The Art of Being**

2. **Doing the Work**

3. **The Haves and Have-Nots**

The Art of Being:

The Biblical Principle of Be Do Have

Let's talk about a principle that's as old as time itself, yet as relevant today as it was thousands of years ago: the Be Do Have principle. This isn't just some catchy phrase; it's a profound truth rooted in biblical wisdom that has the power to transform your life from the inside out.

At its core, the Be Do Have principle is a simple yet powerful formula for success. It states that in order to have the things you desire in life, you must first do the things that are necessary, and to do those things, you must first be the kind of person who is capable of doing them.

Think of it like this: You can't harvest a crop of apples if you haven't planted apple seeds. You can't build a house without first laying the foundation. And you can't achieve your dreams without first becoming the person who is capable of achieving them.

This principle is echoed throughout the Bible, particularly in the teachings of Jesus. In the Gospel of Matthew, Jesus says, "Ask and it will be given to you; seek and you will find; knock and the door will be opened to you." This verse highlights the importance of taking action (asking, seeking, knocking) in order to receive what we desire.

But Jesus also emphasizes the importance of being. In the Sermon on the Mount, he says, "Blessed are the pure in heart, for they will see God." This verse suggests that our inner state of being, our purity of heart, is essential for experiencing the fullness of life.

The Be Do Have principle is not just about achieving material success; it's about becoming the best version of yourself, living a life of purpose and meaning, and making a positive impact on the world.

It's about aligning your actions with your values, your beliefs, and your deepest desires. It's about living a life of integrity, authenticity, and service to others.

Creation and the First Commandment

In Genesis 1:1, we find the foundational elements of creation: time, space, and matter. God established these dimensions as the framework within which all of existence operates. The first commandment given to humanity was to be fruitful and multiply, setting the stage for a life governed by the principles of be, do, and have. Everything we do is governed by this principle, even if we don't always recognize it.

In the beginning, God created the heavens and the earth, laying the foundation of time, space, and matter. These elements form the structure within which all life exists. Just as God laid the foundation for the universe, we must lay the foundation for our own lives by understanding and applying the Be Do Have principle.

The first commandment given to humanity in Genesis 1:28 is to "be fruitful and multiply." This directive is not just about procreation but encompasses all aspects of life. It is a call to increase, to expand, and to grow. The principles of be, do, and have are embedded in this commandment.

1. **Be Fruitful:** To be fruitful means to produce good results, to generate positive outcomes. It starts with being— cultivating the right mindset, values, and character. When you are fruitful in your being, your actions will naturally follow suit.

2. **Do Multiply:** Multiplication is an active process. It requires effort, diligence, and consistency. You must do the work necessary to multiply your efforts, whether it's in your personal growth, relationships, or professional endeavors.

3. **Have Dominion:** Dominion represents the outcomes of your efforts. When you have multiplied your actions, you will naturally have dominion over your life & results. This means achieving your goals and reaping the rewards of your hard work.

The principle of disruption following intention is also crucial here. When you decide to make a positive change in your life, the first thing that shows up is often something hard. This is because disruption follows intention. There is no champion without a challenge. Just like in sports, where the Super Bowl or the NBA playoffs would be meaningless without opponents, the challenges we face make our achievements more valuable.

Consider the analogy of planting a tree. Jim Rohn once said, "God said, plant the seed and I'll make the tree." Aren't you glad He didn't say, "I'll plant the seed and you make the tree. How do you grow a tree"? Just as we don't know how to grow a tree, we don't always know how to produce an outcome. Our role is to plant the seed—to take the necessary actions—and trust that the outcome will follow in due time.

Every deed and action are seeds that we are sowing into the garden of our future. Whether we realize it or not, the choices we make today will shape our tomorrow. This understanding empowers us to take deliberate, positive actions that will lead to the future we desire.

Becoming the Person Who Can Achieve Success

You have to become the person who is capable of doing the things worthy of having success. This concept is rooted in the principle of sowing and reaping: everything you have today is based on seeds you have sown in the past. If you desire a different harvest, you must sow different seeds.

This principle is echoed in many spiritual teachings, including the Bible: "Whatsoever a man soweth, that he shall also reap." The scientific principle of inputs versus outputs aligns with this idea: the quality of your inputs determines the quality of your outputs.

Consider the analogy of planting a tree. Jim Rohn once said, "God said, plant the seed and I'll grow the tree." Aren't you glad He didn't say, "I'll plant the seed and you grow the tree"? Just as we don't know how to grow a tree, we

don't always know how to produce an outcome. Our role is to plant the seed—to take the necessary actions—and trust that the outcome will follow in due time.

Every deed and action are seeds that we are sowing into the garden of our future. Whether we realize it or not, the choices we make today will shape our tomorrow. This understanding empowers us to take deliberate, positive actions that will lead to the future we desire.

Personal self-development is crucial because you have to be getting better every day to prepare yourself for the next day. You must become obsessed with creating the highest version of yourself. When you become more focused on becoming the person capable of achieving your goals rather than the goals themselves, you start to grow.

For instance, if you want to get straight A's, you must first become a disciplined and dedicated student. This means developing effective study habits, managing your time well, and seeking help when needed. If you want to make a million dollars, you must first develop the mindset, skills, and habits of a successful entrepreneur. This involves continuous learning, networking, and resilience.

The desire alone is not enough; you must become the person who can achieve those goals. It's about transforming your identity and aligning your actions with your aspirations. The journey of self-development is ongoing and requires a commitment to lifelong learning and improvement.

High Frequency Chart

Understanding the levels of frequency can help you recognize where you are and where you need to improve. At the top of the chart, you have high-frequency states like enlightenment, peace, joy, love, and acceptance. At the bottom, you have low-frequency states like fear, guilt, and shame. Being in a high-frequency state attracts positive outcomes.

When I was going through a difficult time in my life, I realized that my negative mindset was attracting more negativity. I started focusing on positive growth, taking care of my mind, body, and spirit. I formed positive habits, developed a positive self-image, and gradually moved from a low-frequency state to a high-frequency state. This shift changed my life.

For example, during my struggle with depression, I was constantly in a state of fear and self-doubt. This low-frequency state affected every aspect of my life. When I consciously decided to focus on gratitude, self-love, and positive actions, I noticed a significant improvement in my mental and emotional well-being. This change in frequency attracted better opportunities, relationships, and experiences into my life.

Choosing Your Being

We have the extraordinary power to choose who we are going to be in any given situation. This is our superpower. For example, if someone treats you poorly, we can choose to respond with kindness and understanding rather than anger and resentment. This choice of being loving rather than hateful shapes our actions and ultimately our experiences.

During my struggle with depression, I was being negative, unhealthy, and focused on lack. By choosing to be positive, growth-oriented, and healthy, I transformed my life. I started dressing nicer, going to the gym, and developing positive thought patterns. This shift has led to significant improvements in my life.

Think about it: if you consistently choose to be patient, kind, and proactive, your actions will reflect those qualities. Over time, these actions will lead to positive outcomes. Conversely, if you choose to be negative, reactive, and pessimistic, your actions will mirror those traits, resulting in less desirable outcomes.

Doing the Work:

The importance of consistent effort and dedication.

Success doesn't happen overnight. It's a marathon that requires consistent effort, unwavering dedication, and a whole lot of grit. Every successful person has put in the work day in and day out. They embrace the grind, knowing that it's all part of the journey. Think about athletes, entrepreneurs, or artists. They didn't just dream about their goals; they chased them relentlessly. They got up early, worked through challenges, and pushed themselves daily. They embraced the process, the journey, and the grind.

For example, consider a professional athlete like a marathon runner. They didn't become elite athletes overnight. They trained consistently, pushing their limits and improving their performance bit by bit. They faced setbacks, injuries, and tough competition, but their dedication and perseverance paid off in the end. The same principle applies to any field. Entrepreneurs who build successful businesses often spend years perfecting their products, understanding their markets, and building relationships. Artists who achieve mastery dedicate countless hours to honing their craft, learning from every failure and success along the way.

To succeed, you must be willing to commit to the process, no matter how long it takes. This means showing up every day, ready to work, even when you don't feel like it. It means embracing the hard times and pushing through the challenges. It means being persistent and never giving up, no matter how many times you fail. Success is not a destination but a journey, and it is the consistent effort and dedication that ultimately lead to achievement.

Developing discipline and focus.

Discipline and focus are the unsung heroes of success. They are the muscles of your mind that need to be trained and strengthened over time. The more you exercise them, the stronger they become. Without discipline and focus, it's easy to get sidetracked and lose sight of your goals. With them, you can maintain a steady course and make continuous progress.

Here are a few strategies to develop discipline and focus:

1. **Set Clear Goals:** Know what you're working towards. Clear, specific goals provide direction and motivation. When you have a clear goal in mind, it's easier to stay focused and disciplined because you know what you are aiming for.

2. **Create a Routine:** Routines provide structure and predictability, making it easier to stay on track. A well-established routine helps you manage your time effectively and ensures that you dedicate enough time to the tasks that matter most.

3. **Break Tasks into Smaller Chunks:** Large tasks can be overwhelming. Breaking them into smaller, manageable steps makes them more achievable. This approach helps you make steady progress without feeling overwhelmed.

4. **Eliminate Distractions:** Turn off notifications, close unnecessary tabs, and find a quiet place to work.

Minimizing distractions helps maintain focus. When you eliminate distractions, you can concentrate fully on your work and achieve better results.

5. **Practice Mindfulness:** Mindfulness techniques, such as meditation, can improve concentration and reduce stress. Mindfulness helps you stay present and focused, which is crucial for maintaining discipline.

6. **Reward Yourself**: Celebrate your successes, no matter how small. Rewards reinforce positive behavior and keep you motivated. Recognizing your achievements helps you stay motivated and encourages you to continue working hard.

Discipline and focus are like muscles that require regular exercise. Just as you wouldn't expect to build physical strength without consistent workouts, you can't develop mental discipline without regular practice. Over time, these practices become habits that support your success. When you cultivate discipline and focus, you create a strong foundation for achieving your goals and realizing your potential.

Overcoming procrastination and self-doubt.

Procrastination and self-doubt are the twin evils that lurk in the shadows of our minds. They are the silent killers of ambition. To overcome them, you must acknowledge the problem, set small, achievable goals, use a timer to stay focused, keep your word to yourself, practice positive self-talk, surround yourself with driven people, and seek guidance from mentors.

Procrastination often stems from a fear of failure or a lack of confidence. By setting small, achievable goals, you can build momentum and confidence. For example, when I was struggling with self-doubt, I started practicing positive self-talk and affirmations. I reminded myself of my strengths and past successes. I also sought guidance from mentors who had overcome similar challenges. Their support and wisdom helped me stay focused and motivated.

Self-doubt can be paralyzing, but it's important to remember that everyone experiences it at some point. The key is to recognize it and take steps to counteract it. Positive self-talk, affirmations, and surrounding yourself with supportive people can make a significant difference. Seek out mentors and role models who can provide guidance and encouragement. Their experiences and insights can help you navigate your own challenges and build confidence in your abilities.

The power of habits and routines in achieving goals.

Habits are the building blocks of our lives. They shape our days and ultimately our destinies. By cultivating positive habits and routines, we can create a life of excellence. Habits are powerful because they automate behavior, allowing us to perform tasks with minimal effort and thought. By developing good habits, you can create a strong foundation for success.

Consider the analogy of compound interest. Just as small, consistent investments can grow into substantial wealth over time, small, positive habits can lead to significant changes in your life. For example, developing the habit of exercising daily can lead to improved health and increased energy levels. Over time, these benefits compound, leading to a healthier, more energetic, and more productive life.

Start by identifying a few key habits that align with your goals. For instance, if you want to improve your physical health, commit to a daily exercise routine, eating nutritious meals, and getting adequate sleep. Over time, these habits will compound, leading to significant improvements in your overall well-being.

Creating a routine is also crucial. Routines provide structure and consistency, making it easier to maintain good habits. A well-established routine helps you manage your time effectively and ensures that you dedicate enough time to the tasks that matter most. When your daily actions align with your long-term goals, you create a powerful synergy that propels you toward success.

Extreme Dedication and Positive Daily Actions

To achieve greatness, never take a day off. Extreme dedication and obsession with your goals are key. Engage in positive daily actions, starting by getting up early. Use that quiet time in the morning—whether it's 5 AM or 4 AM—for prayer, meditation, and journaling. This is what I call my time with God. Read something of wisdom, even if it's just a page or two from the Bible, a self-help book, or something inspiring. Get into the flow.

Getting up early provides a head start on the day. The quiet of the early morning hours allows you to focus and prepare mentally and spiritually for the challenges ahead. Use this time for self-reflection, setting intentions, and planning your day. This practice helps you start the day with a clear mind and a sense of purpose.

Get an early workout in—run, walk, lift, hike, or box. Different forms of exercise provide new challenges and help you grow. Physical activity boosts your energy levels, improves your mood, and enhances your overall well-being. By incorporating regular exercise into your routine, you set yourself up for a productive and successful day.

Then, get to work on your top priorities. Whether you're a student, athlete, or business professional, focus on the tasks that will push you forward. Prioritize your most important tasks and tackle them first. This approach ensures that you make progress on your key goals every day.

Adopt healthy eating habits. Get your macros, drink spring water and the right nutrients. Based on science, nutrition, and biblical principles, I don't eat unclean foods like pork, shrimp, crabs, and lobsters. I try to avoid bread, carbs, and sugar and I don't eat fast food. Focus on clean meats, fruits, and vegetables. This approach helps you think clearly, have more energy, and perform optimally.

Healthy eating is a cornerstone of a productive and successful life. The right nutrients fuel your body and mind, allowing you to perform at your best. By making conscious choices about what you eat, you can enhance your physical health, mental clarity, and overall well-being.

Challenging Negative Self-Talk and Delaying Gratification

Constantly challenge your negative self-talk. Replace social media with reading books, TV and Netflix with podcasts, and music with audiobooks or silence. Spend time outdoors in the sun and prioritize what's most important: your family, health, and finances.

Negative self-talk can be a major obstacle to success. It undermines your confidence and prevents you from reaching your full potential. By challenging negative thoughts and replacing them with positive affirmations, you can build a more positive and resilient mindset.

Delaying gratification is another important skill. It's easy to get caught up in the pursuit of immediate pleasure, but true success often requires sacrificing short-term comfort for long-term gain. By focusing on your long-term goals and making consistent efforts to achieve them, you can create a life of lasting fulfillment.

Follow the commandments of God and the laws of nature. These principles are designed for us to win and flourish. We are one with nature and God. How we treat ourselves reflects on how we treat others. This approach guides us on how to lead, gain wisdom, and create generational wealth.

If you genuinely try your best all the time, every day, it is impossible to fail. God rewards those who strive to become greater and more godlike. By living in alignment with God, your values and following a disciplined, dedicated approach to your goals, you can achieve success and make a positive impact on the world around you.

The Haves and Have-Nots:

Principles of Sowing and Reaping

The principle of sowing and reaping states that what you sow, you shall reap. This applies to all areas of life. If you plant apple seeds, you're not going to harvest oranges. If you sow kindness, you're not going to reap animosity.

This principle is about inputs and outputs. The quality of what you put into your efforts directly affects the quality of what you get out. This concept is rooted in both natural law and spiritual teachings. For example, in Galatians 6:7, it is written, "Do not be deceived: God cannot be mocked. A man reaps what he sows."

Think about your daily actions as seeds. Every kind word, every moment of hard work, every act of generosity is a seed planted in the garden of your future. These seeds will grow and eventually yield a harvest that reflects your efforts and intentions.

Developing an Abundance Mindset

The "haves" and "have-nots" are not merely defined by material possessions, but by their mindsets and perspectives. The "haves" possess an abundance mindset, a deep-seated belief in the limitless possibilities and opportunities that life has to offer. The "have-nots," on the other hand, are trapped in a scarcity mindset, a belief that there's never enough to go around, that resources are limited, and that they are destined to struggle.

The good news is that your mindset is not fixed. It's a choice, a conscious decision you make every day. You can choose to focus on lack and limitation, or you can choose to embrace abundance and possibility. And the key to unlocking this abundance mindset lies in the power of gratitude.

Gratitude is more than just saying "thank you." It's a way of life, a conscious choice to focus on the good in your life, and take care of it, no matter how small or insignificant it may seem. It's about appreciating the present moment, recognizing the blessings that surround you, and cultivating a sense of contentment and joy.

When you practice gratitude, you shift your focus from what you lack to what you have. You begin to see the world through a lens of abundance, recognizing the limitless opportunities and possibilities that are available to you.

This shift in perspective can have a profound impact on your life. When you believe that there is enough for everyone, you open yourself up to receiving more. You attract abundance into your life, not just in the form of material wealth, but also in the form of love, joy, peace, and fulfillment.

Overcoming scarcity mindset and limiting beliefs

Let's talk about money, honey. Or rather, let's talk about our relationship with money. It's a topic that's often shrouded in shame, guilt, and limiting beliefs. We're told that money is the root of all evil, that it's selfish to desire wealth, that we should be content with what we have.

But what if I told you that these beliefs are holding you back from achieving your full potential? What if I told you that you can have a healthy, abundant relationship with money, one that empowers you to create a life of freedom, impact, and generosity?

The first step is to recognize and overcome the scarcity mindset. This is the belief that there's not enough to go around, that resources are limited, and that someone else's gain is your loss. It's a mindset rooted in fear, lack, and competition.

When we operate from a scarcity mindset, we constantly feel like we're not enough, that we don't have enough, and that we'll never have enough. This mindset can manifest in various ways, such as:

1. **Hoarding**: Clinging tightly to what you have, afraid to spend or share, because you fear there won't be more.

2. **Comparison**: Constantly comparing yourself to others, feeling envious of their success and resentful of their abundance.

3. **Lack of Generosity** Hesitating to give to others, whether it's your time, money, or talents, because you believe you don't have enough to spare.

4. **Fear of Taking Risks:** Avoiding risks or pursuing dreams because you fear failure and the potential loss of resources.

The scarcity mindset is a self-fulfilling prophecy. When we believe there's not enough, we act in ways that create scarcity. We hoard, we compete, we withhold, and we miss out on opportunities for growth and abundance.

But there's another way. It's called the abundance mindset. This is the belief that there's more than enough to go around, that resources are infinite, and that everyone can thrive. It's a mindset rooted in gratitude, generosity, and collaboration.

When we operate from an abundance mindset, we feel empowered, grateful, and optimistic about the future. We see opportunities everywhere, we're willing to share our resources, and we're not afraid to take risks.

Building a legacy and leaving a positive impact

The Be Do Have principle isn't just about personal gain; it's about creating a ripple effect of positivity that extends far beyond ourselves. It's about building a legacy that will outlive us, a legacy that inspires and uplifts others.

Think of the people you admire most, the ones who have left an indelible mark on the world. What is it about them that resonates with you? Is it their wealth, their fame, their power? Or is it something deeper, something more meaningful?

I believe that true legacy is not measured by material possessions or fleeting accolades. It's measured by the impact we have on others, the lives we touch, the difference we make in the world.

Building a legacy is not about self-aggrandizement; it's about service to others. It's about using our unique gifts and talents to make a positive contribution to society. It's about leaving the world a better place than we found it.

So, how can we build a legacy that will stand the test of time? How can we leave a positive impact on the world?

1. **Start with Yourself:** The foundation of any legacy is a strong sense of self. You must first become the person you want to be remembered as. This means cultivating your character, developing your skills, and living a life of integrity and purpose.

2. **Find Your Passion:** What are you passionate about? What gets you excited, what makes you feel alive? Your passion is your unique gift to the world, and it's through your passion that you can make the greatest impact.

3. **Serve Others:** Legacy is not about what you get; it's about what you give. Look for ways to use your talents and skills to serve others. Volunteer your time, mentor young people, donate to causes you care about. The more you give, the more you'll receive in return.

4. **Be a Lifelong Learner:** The world is constantly changing, and so should you. Never stop learning, growing, and evolving. The more knowledge and skills you acquire, the more value you can offer to the world.

5. **Build Relationships:** Your relationships are your greatest asset. Invest in your family, your friends, your colleagues, and your community. The stronger your relationships, the greater your impact.

6. **Leave a Mark:** Think about the kind of mark you want to leave on the world. What do you want to be remembered

for? Write down your goals, your dreams, your aspirations. Then, take action to make them a reality.

7. **Be a Mentor:** Share your knowledge and experience with others. Mentor young people, guide them on their journey, and help them to reach their full potential.

Building a legacy requires intentionality and commitment. It's about living with purpose and making choices that reflect your values and aspirations. By focusing on the impact you want to make and taking consistent actions towards that vision, you can create a lasting legacy that inspires and uplifts others.

In conclusion, the Be Do Have principle is a powerful framework for personal and professional growth. It emphasizes the importance of being, doing, and having in that order. By becoming the person capable of achieving your goals, taking consistent action towards those goals, and cultivating a mindset of abundance and gratitude, you can create a life of fulfillment and success. Remember, the journey is just as important as the destination. Embrace the process, learn from the challenges, and celebrate your progress along the way.

Summary

In this raw and unfiltered account of my life, we've journeyed together through the highs and lows, the triumphs and setbacks, the moments of despair and the glimmers of hope. We've explored the depths of my experiences, from the challenges of growing up in a financially disadvantaged household to the devastating losses that shook me to my core.

We've delved into the transformative power of personal development, the unwavering support of faith, and the importance of cultivating a positive mindset. We've discussed the significance of taking risks, embracing challenges, and pushing beyond our comfort zones. We've explored the principles of sowing and reaping, the importance of giving and serving others, and the power of gratitude and abundance mindset.

Throughout this journey, we've witnessed the resilience of the human spirit, the capacity for growth and transformation, and the unwavering belief in the power of the individual to overcome adversity and achieve greatness.

The transformative power of self-belief, resilience, and purpose.

One of the key takeaways from my story is the transformative power of self-belief, resilience, and purpose. When we believe in ourselves, we tap into a wellspring of inner strength and determination. We become unstoppable, capable of achieving anything we set our minds to.

Resilience, the ability to bounce back from setbacks and challenges, is another essential ingredient for success. It's not about avoiding adversity, but about facing it head-on, learning from it, and emerging stronger on the other side.

And purpose, the driving force behind our actions, gives our lives meaning and direction. When we live a life that is aligned with our values, passions, and unique gifts, we tap into a source of fulfillment and joy that is both deep and enduring.

The importance of taking action and applying the lessons learned

But self-belief, resilience, and purpose are not enough. We must also take action, apply the lessons we've learned, and make conscious choices that move us closer to our goals. It's not about waiting for the perfect moment or the perfect opportunity; it's about taking the first step, even when it's scary or uncertain.

Remember, knowledge is not power; it's potential power. It's only when we apply what we've learned that we truly transform our lives. So, take the tools and strategies you've gained from this book and put them into practice. Experiment, explore, and discover what works best for you.

Encouragement to continue the journey of personal growth and self-discovery.

The journey of personal growth and self-discovery is a lifelong adventure. It's not a destination, but a continuous process of learning, evolving, and becoming the best version of yourself.

So, I encourage you to embrace this journey with open arms. Don't be afraid to step outside of your comfort zone, to challenge your beliefs, and to explore new possibilities. Surround yourself with positive and supportive people, seek out mentors who can guide you, and never stop learning and growing.

Remember, you are capable of achieving anything you set your mind to. You are worthy of love, happiness, and success. And you have a unique contribution to make to the world.

So, go out there and make your mark. Live a life that is true to yourself, a life that is filled with passion, purpose, and meaning. This is your journey, and I'm honored to have been a part of it.

ACKNOWLEDGMENTS

First and foremost, I express my deepest gratitude to God, whose grace and guidance have been the cornerstone of my journey. Your unwavering presence and love have been my guiding light through every challenge and triumph. Without you I am nothing.

To my Mom, Dad, and four sisters, thank you for your endless love, support, and belief in me. Your encouragement has fueled my determination and inspired me to push beyond my limits.

I am immensely grateful to my entire family for their unwavering support and understanding throughout my journey. Your love has been a source of strength and comfort during the toughest of times.

To all the people closest to me who have witnessed my struggles and growth, thank you for standing by my side and believing in me even when I doubted myself. Your presence in my life has been a blessing beyond measure.

I want to acknowledge and express my gratitude to the mentors who have played pivotal roles in shaping my path and guiding me towards self-discovery and personal growth. Your insights have illuminated my path and empowered me to become the best version of myself.

Special thanks to countless others whose teachings have profoundly impacted my journey of self-discovery and growth.

To all those whom I have lost along the way, your presence in my life, no matter how brief, has left an indelible mark on my soul. Your memories continue to inspire me to live each day with purpose and gratitude.

Thank you to each and every individual who has played a role, big or small, in shaping me into the person I am today. Your support, guidance, and love have been instrumental in my journey, and I am forever grateful.

ABOUT THE HARRY JONES GROUP LLC,

The Harry Jones Group is more than just an education company; it's a movement aimed at empowering the youth and people across the globe to unlock their full potential. Founded by Harry Jones III, the Harry Jones Group is dedicated to providing resources and tools for personal growth, emotional resilience, career pathways and success in life. Through an innovative online education platform, engaging books, impactful masterminds, and speaking engagements, The Harry Jones Group is committed to equipping the next generation and individuals worldwide with the skills and mindset needed to thrive in today's world.

At the heart of The Harry Jones Group is a mission to inspire positive change and transformation. By sharing his own journey of overcoming adversity, Harry encourages others to embrace their challenges as opportunities for growth and to cultivate a mindset of resilience and determination. Whether speaking to students in schools, leading workshops, or developing cutting-edge educational resources, The Harry Jones Group seeks to empower people of all ages and backgrounds to reach new heights and achieve their dreams.

Made in the USA
Middletown, DE
03 September 2024

59684156R00109